I0813253

Presented to

From

Date

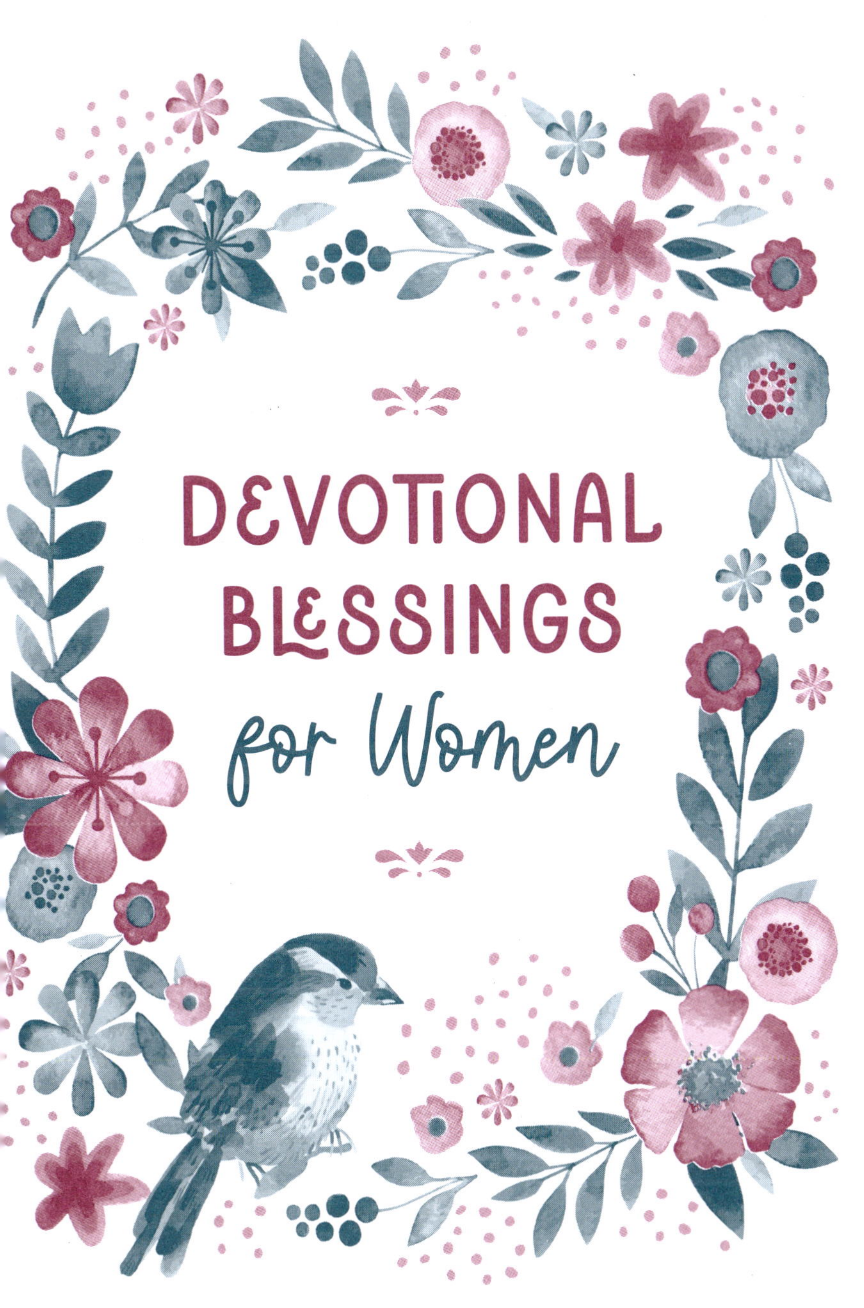
DEVOTIONAL
BLESSINGS
for Women

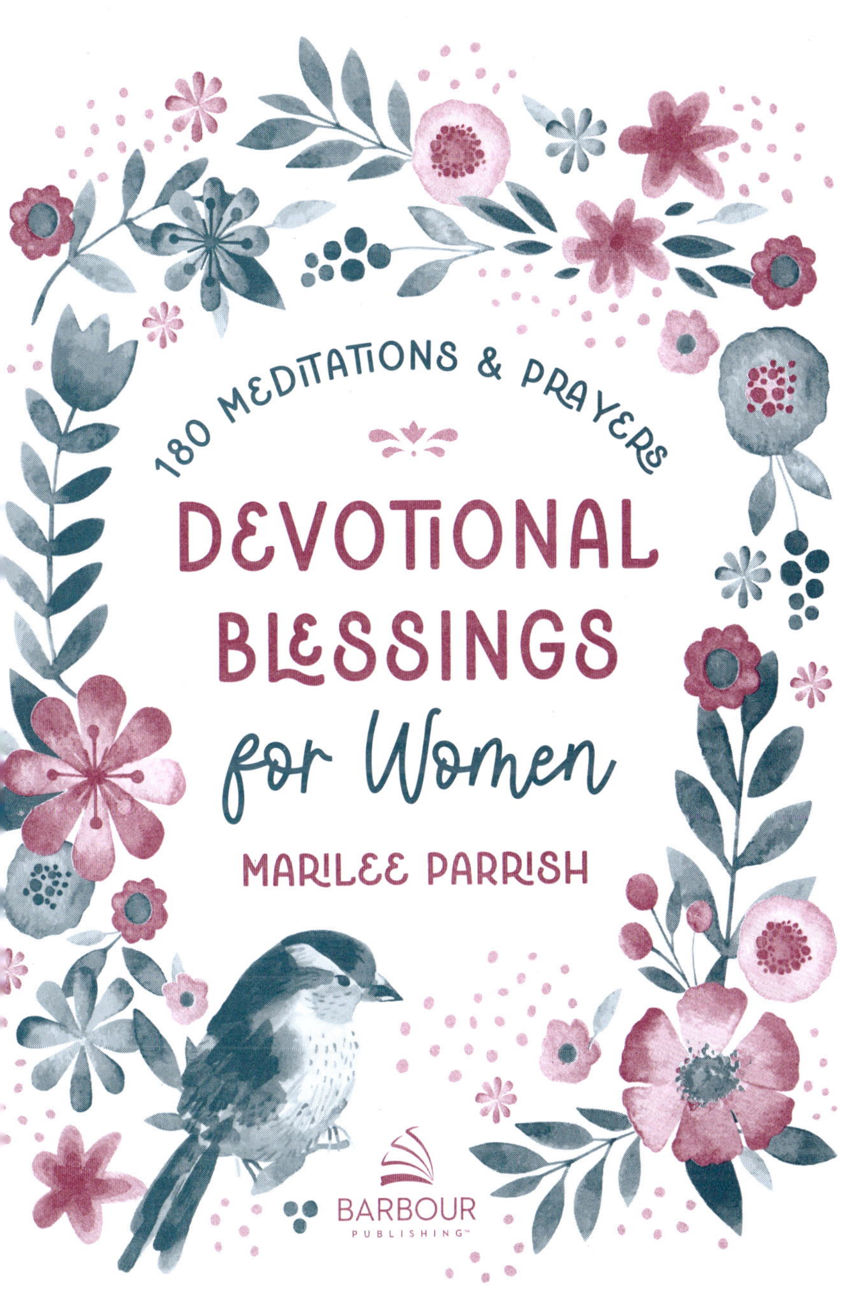

180 MEDITATIONS & PRAYERS

DEVOTIONAL BLESSINGS for Women

MARILEE PARRISH

BARBOUR PUBLISHING™

YOU are the reason we do what we do here at Barbour Publishing. We promise that we will always use our God-given talents to produce content with you in mind—and that we will remain biblically faithful, no matter what.

Thank you for being the heart of our business.

Print ISBN 979-8-89151-266-5

Published by Barbour Publishing, Inc., 1810 Barbour Drive, Uhrichsville, Ohio 44683, www.barbourbooks.com

Our mission is to inspire the world with the life-changing message of the Bible.

Printed in India.

Blessings Are Yours, *dear one!*

God wants to bless you. He really does. You may feel undeserving or that you must earn His blessing, but that's not His way.

The Bible literally tells us that Jesus loves us in the same way that God the Father loves Him! John 15:9 (AMP) says: "I have loved you just as the Father has loved Me; remain in My love [and do not doubt My love for you]."

Jesus died for you. Paid the ultimate sacrifice so you could be free, once and for all. And yet He still shows up in everyday ways over and over again, surprising us with His love.

But me he caught—reached all the way from sky to sea; he pulled me out of that ocean of hate, that enemy chaos, the void in which I was drowning. They hit me when I was down, but God stuck by me. He stood me up on a wide-open field; I stood there saved—surprised to be loved!

Psalm 18:16–19 MSG

Lord God, Your written Word tells us that Your goodness and unfailing love will pursue us all the days of our lives (Psalm 23:6). We rest in the truth of Your great promise!

THE SAME LOVE

"I have made Your name known to them and will make it known. So then the love You have for Me may be in them and I may be in them."

JOHN 17:26 NLV

Jesus prayed that the same love that God the Father has for His Son, Jesus, would be in you. What a miraculous mystery that the God of heaven comes to make His home in our hearts (John 14:23)! The Bible has so much to say about how loved and blessed you are as a child of God. You are the dwelling place of God's Spirit. The same love that exists between God the Father and Jesus the Son is what is alive and at work in you!

Let that truth sink in.

If you've grown up in church, it can be easy to start believing that God's love is for everyone else. . .and forget that His deep and unfailing love is meant for you too. How are you doing at receiving God's love for you today?

Jesus, search my heart. Show me anything that might be getting in the way of my ability to receive Your love today. Wash me afresh in Your gracious love.

FOR GOD SO LOVED

For God so loved the world that he gave his one and only Son, that whoever believes in him shall not perish but have eternal life. For God did not send his Son into the world to condemn the world, but to save the world through him.

JOHN 3:16–17 NIV

Let the simple yet profound truth of John 3:16 wash over you again. It is so simple that a child can accept it, yet so profound that it changes everything!

Jesus has all authority and power over all things. Why is this so important? It means that you can go to Jesus with all your questions. It means that He has authority over everything that might come your way in this life. It means that He is bigger than all your problems, failures, and fears. And you have access to this power at every moment because He is alive in you, constantly reminding you of His truth and His great love for you!

Jesus, I put my trust in You alone. I accept the truth of Your Word. I believe You have come not to condemn me but to offer me an abundant life with You—now and forever.

THE BLESSING OF HIS PRESENCE

You make known to me the path of life; you will fill me with joy in your presence, with eternal pleasures at your right hand.

Psalm 16:11 NIV

God promises to bless you with joy as you spend time in His presence. You have access to His peace, joy, and presence right now and forever. The Holy Spirit alive inside of you will show you the way.

Hebrews 4:15–16 (MSG) says, "We don't have a priest who is out of touch with our reality. He's been through weakness and testing, experienced it all—all but the sin. So let's walk right up to him and get what he is so ready to give."

Because of what Jesus has done for you, you are always welcome in God's presence. He will never turn you away. You can walk right up to Him and lift your head. He sees you. He knows your heart. He knows the struggles you face. He wants to help carry your load and give you peace.

God, I want the blessing of Your constant presence in my life. Thank You for the peace and joy that only You can give.

NOTHING GREATER

"No one has greater love [nor stronger commitment] than to lay down his own life for his friends."
JOHN 15:13 AMP

Have you ever thought about God's commitment to you? God lavishly loves you *and* He is eternally committed to you. He wants the best for you. He won't give up on you. He will never fail you. And He will finish what He started in you.

Philippians 1:6 (AMP) says, "I am convinced and confident of this very thing, that He who has begun a good work in you will [continue to] perfect and complete it until the day of Christ Jesus [the time of His return]."

In your search for love in this life, you'll find that nothing is greater than the unfailing love that God has for you. Rest in that truth. It is a faithful, enduring, and committed love. It can't be earned. It was given at your lowest point. And there's nothing you can ever do to make God love you any more or any less than He does right now.

Lord God, thank You for Your amazing and undeserved gift of love.

THE BLESSING OF CORRECTION

See what great love the Father has lavished on us, that we should be called children of God! And that is what we are!

1 John 3:1 niv

Our great God is a good Dad. You may struggle with the way you were parented or with your own parenting fails. . .but God parents perfectly. He always welcomes you with love and grace, even when you've made a mistake. His correction is clear and kind, His discipline loving and hope-filled.

He doesn't shame you. The Bible tells us in Romans 2:4 that it is God's loving-kindness that brings us to repentance. Hebrews 12:4–11 (msg) helps us understand this better: "Only irresponsible parents leave children to fend for themselves. Would you prefer an irresponsible God? We respect our own parents for training and not spoiling us, so why not embrace God's training so we can truly live? While we were children, our parents did what seemed best to them. But God is doing what is best for us, training us to live God's holy best."

Thank You for parenting me perfectly, Father God. Help me embrace the blessing of Your correction.

HIGHER WAYS

"For my thoughts are not your thoughts, neither are your ways my ways," declares the LORD. "As the heavens are higher than the earth, so are my ways higher than your ways and my thoughts than your thoughts."

ISAIAH 55:8–9 NIV

Thank God, He doesn't think and act like humans do! When we're ready to give up, He doesn't. When we run out of patience, He endures. He never gets it wrong. And He always looks at us with love because of everything Jesus did for us on the cross.

Take a look at what the Bible says:

- "The LORD passed before him and proclaimed, 'The LORD, the LORD, a God merciful and gracious, slow to anger, and abounding in steadfast love and faithfulness'" (Exodus 34:6 ESV).
- "But you, O Lord, are a God merciful and gracious, slow to anger and abounding in steadfast love and faithfulness" (Psalm 86:15 ESV).

Our God is full of mercy, grace, steadfast love, and faithfulness. You are welcomed and valued in His sight.

God, I'm so amazed that I am welcome in Your presence. Thank You for Your unwavering faithfulness and overwhelming love.

WHOLE AND HOLY

But now, by giving himself completely at the Cross, actually dying for you, Christ brought you over to God's side and put your lives together, whole and holy in his presence. You don't walk away from a gift like that! You stay grounded and steady in that bond of trust, constantly tuned in to the Message, careful not to be distracted or diverted.

COLOSSIANS 1:22 MSG

Because of the work of Christ for you on the cross, you are whole and holy in God's sight. This is a completely undeserved gift of grace for all who believe.

Those guilty feelings you have of not being or doing enough? Let them go. Those feelings of shame about your past? Lift your head. Messages from the enemy that this couldn't possibly be true for you? Command them to leave in Jesus' name.

Jesus died to make you whole and holy. He is committed to seeing His work through in you. Take a deep breath and relax in the truth that God Himself is holding your hand on this journey.

Lord God, please steady my heart in the truth of Your Word. I am whole and holy in Your presence.

THE BLESSING OF HIS WORD

He brought me to the banqueting house,
and his banner over me was love.
Song of Songs 2:4 ESV

God has treasures and blessings waiting for you in each new day. Take a moment to ask Him to open your spiritual eyes to see His treasures. One of the ways He wants to bless you is through His Word. Ask Him to give you a deep desire to get to know Him better in this way. A new habit to consider is to look up your daily scriptures in multiple Bible versions. This practice helps you get a deeper look at the meaning behind the scripture. For example, today's verse in the Amplified Bible says this: "He has brought me to his banqueting place, and his banner over me is love [waving overhead to protect and comfort me]."

By seeing this scripture in a new light, we understand better that God's banner of love is meant to protect and comfort us. As you dig deeper into scripture, the treasures you'll find will bless you in abundant ways. Every piece of scripture is meant to point to Jesus and His unfailing love for you.

God, please fill me with a desire and love for Your Word.

PRAYING GOD'S WORD

Let them give thanks to the LORD for his unfailing love and his wonderful deeds for mankind.

PSALM 107:8 NIV

There is something powerful about praying from God's Word. Let this scripture from Ephesians 3:14–21 (NIV) be on your heart and in your prayers today:

> *For this reason I kneel before the Father, from whom every family in heaven and on earth derives its name. I pray that out of his glorious riches he may strengthen you with power through his Spirit in your inner being, so that Christ may dwell in your hearts through faith. And I pray that you, being rooted and established in love, may have power, together with all the Lord's holy people, to grasp how wide and long and high and deep is the love of Christ, and to know this love that surpasses knowledge—that you may be filled to the measure of all the fullness of God. Now to him who is able to do immeasurably more than all we ask or imagine, according to his power that is at work within us, to him be glory in the church and in Christ Jesus throughout all generations, for ever and ever! Amen.*

ALIVE THROUGH HIM

This is how God showed his love among us: He sent his one and only Son into the world that we might live through him. This is love: not that we loved God, but that he loved us and sent his Son as an atoning sacrifice for our sins. Dear friends, since God so loved us, we also ought to love one another.

1 John 4:9–11 NIV

Jesus came for you so that you might come alive through Him. In Luke 4:18–19 (NIV), hear these words from Jesus Himself: "The Spirit of the Lord is on me, because he has anointed me to proclaim good news to the poor. He has sent me to proclaim freedom for the prisoners and recovery of sight for the blind, to set the oppressed free, to proclaim the year of the Lord's favor."

Jesus came to bring you healing and freedom from sin and death. He also came to bring you abundant life through Him right now (John 10:10). No doubt, life is hard. But you don't have to go it alone. Jesus is with you, carrying your burdens and breathing new life into you moment by moment.

Jesus, breathe new life into me this day as I follow You.

A LOVE THAT LASTS FOREVER

But God clearly shows and proves His own love for us, by the fact that while we were still sinners, Christ died for us.
ROMANS 5:8 AMP

Look at these amazing verses that tell us how much God loves us:

- "This is love! It is not that we loved God but that He loved us. For God sent His Son to pay for our sins with His own blood" (1 John 4:10 NLV).
- "The Lord came to us from far away, saying, 'I have loved you with a love that lasts forever. So I have helped you come to Me with loving-kindness'" (Jeremiah 31:3 NLV).
- "And hope does not put us to shame, because God's love has been poured out into our hearts through the Holy Spirit, who has been given to us" (Romans 5:5 NIV).

And those are just a few! God's Word is full of evidence that shows how much He loves you. It is the only perfect love that lasts forever.

Lord God, thank You for Your perfect, forever love. I don't deserve it, but I'm so thankful!

A NEVER-ENDING SUPPLY

Place me like a seal over your heart, like a seal on your arm. . . .
Many waters cannot quench love, nor can rivers drown it.
SONG OF SONGS 8:6–7 NLT

Are you in the daily habit of waking up with thankfulness in your heart? Allowing God's love to wash over you and saturate every part of your being each morning can change the way you relate to God, yourself, and others. He gives love from a never-ending supply, and that same love is alive in you. . .allowing you to give love from that same never-ending supply. But if you're waking up empty because you've allowed yourself to become fully depleted, that emptiness will take its toll.

The truth is that a mighty resurrection power lives in you through Christ. He fills you to overflowing with His power so that you can love and be loved. So that you can live and breathe and serve.

When you rely on your own strength, forgetting God in the process, you'll find how quickly and repeatedly you run out of resources.

Jesus, forgive me for depending on my own strength.
Place a desire in my heart to come to You for
everything I need to love You and others well.

CHRIST LIVES IN ME

I have been crucified with Christ and I no longer live, but Christ lives in me. The life I now live in the body, I live by faith in the Son of God, who loved me and gave himself for me.

GALATIANS 2:20 NIV

The Holy Spirit helps us accomplish two very important things: (1) loving God and (2) keeping His commandments!

Read these words: "Spiritually alive, we have access to everything God's Spirit is doing, and can't be judged by unspiritual critics. Isaiah's question, 'Is there anyone around who knows God's Spirit, anyone who knows what he is doing?' has been answered: Christ knows, and we have Christ's Spirit" (1 Corinthians 2:15–16 MSG).

When we have the Spirit of Jesus alive in us, we experience transformation, God's Word is brought to life in us, we begin to understand things we couldn't before, and we are taught by Jesus Himself.

I'm so thankful for the powerful and victorious life You've planned for me! Thank You, Jesus!

ALONE WITH GOD

The earth, O Lord, is full of Your lovingkindness and goodness; teach me Your statutes.
Psalm 119:64 AMP

It's so easy to get overwhelmed with life and all the activities and pressures of the world we live in. Sometimes life gets so noisy, it's hard to hear from God. Your life may be filled with good things: family, friends, ministry. . .but it can still be too much at times. When you're feeling the weight of the world on your shoulders, it's time to get alone with God.

The Bible says that the earth is filled with the Lord's goodness, and it definitely can be easier to hear from God in nature. Take a drive through the country. Head to a lake or river with a blanket and your Bible. . .whatever you need to do to block out the distractions and be alone with God. Open your Bible to Matthew 11:28–30 and allow the voice of Jesus to be the loudest one you hear.

God, thank You for this precious time with You. I need Your voice, Your love, and Your strength.

THE SECRET OF BEING CONTENT

I know what it is to be in need, and I know what it is to have plenty. I have learned the secret of being content in any and every situation, whether well fed or hungry, whether living in plenty or in want.

PHILIPPIANS 4:12 NIV

So what's the secret? The answer is found in the very next verse: "I can do all this through him who gives me strength" (Philippians 4:13 NIV). The Message says it this way: "Whatever I have, wherever I am, I can make it through anything in the One who makes me who I am."

Philippians 4:13 is often used as an encouragement to get something done well. It's used before sporting events or physical challenges or important tests that need taken. But this verse is really referring to the fact that we can be content in every situation because of Christ's strength at work in us.

Do you need Christ's strength to be more content in your current situation? Talk to Him about it today.

Jesus, I confess my lack of contentment in this area: ______________. Please fill me with Your strength.

BLESSED BY SERVING

"Now that you know these things, you will be blessed if you do them."
JOHN 13:17 NIV

Jesus and His disciples were preparing to have dinner together on one of the last days before His death. Jesus shocked His followers by going around the room and washing each disciple's feet. That was what servants did. Simon Peter resisted at first. But Jesus wanted to teach them all that the best leader is a humble servant of his people.

John 13:3–4 (NIV) says, "Jesus knew that the Father had put all things under his power, and that he had come from God and was returning to God; so he got up from the meal, took off his outer clothing, and wrapped a towel around his waist."

Jesus knew exactly who He was and had no problem lowering Himself to the place of a servant. When you know who you are in Christ, you can serve others faithfully too. And Jesus says you'll be blessed if you do that.

Lord Jesus, help me to follow Your example in serving others. I trust what You say about me. Give me the courage to be humble like You.

THE LORD BLESS YOU

"The Lord bless you and keep you; the Lord make his face to shine upon you and be gracious to you; the Lord lift up his countenance upon you and give you peace."

Numbers 6:24–26 ESV

Do you ever struggle with feeling like something bad is going to happen or the other shoe is about to drop? Take these thoughts captive and bring them into the presence of God. Ask Him to exchange any lies you may be believing with His truth.

What does this look like in everyday life? Consider this example: You begin to think that bad things are just around the corner for you. Invite Jesus into this thought process you're having. Ask Him if what you're believing is a lie. If it is, ask for His truth to be made known to you. Many times a scripture or worship song will come to mind at this time—for example, Jeremiah 29:11–13 or Romans 8:28. As you refute the lies of the enemy with scriptural truth, your heart and mind become aligned with Christ.

Jesus, please help me take my thoughts captive and make them obedient to Your truth.

THE RICHES OF HIS GLORY

And my God will meet all your needs according to the riches of his glory in Christ Jesus.

PHILIPPIANS 4:19 NIV

Everything is possible when you go to God in prayer. He knows your every need, and the Bible promises that He will meet them. Nothing is too hard for Him. Nothing is out of His realm of possibility. He is the Creator of all, and He cares about you!

Psalm 50:10 (NLT) says, "For all the animals of the forest are mine, and I own the cattle on a thousand hills." God owns it all. And He gives and takes away. The all-powerful God of creation is available to you at every moment, and He wants to bless you with the riches of His glory. He wants you to come to Him and share your heart, your thoughts, your needs, your dreams, your concerns. . .everything.

As you learn to go to Him more and more, the blessing of His presence will always be enough to meet every need you have.

Jesus, I'm amazed that You care so much about me. Thank You for meeting all my needs.

WRAPPED INTO CHRIST

Praise be to the God and Father of our Lord Jesus Christ, who has blessed us in the heavenly realms with every spiritual blessing in Christ.

EPHESIANS 1:3 NIV

The Passion Translation says it this way: "Every spiritual blessing in the heavenly realm has already been lavished upon us as a love gift from our wonderful heavenly Father, the Father of our Lord Jesus—all because he sees us wrapped into Christ. This is why we celebrate him with all our hearts!"

What an astounding blessing that we can walk in the truth of who we are in Christ in every moment! It's a choice you'll have to make every day: to see yourself as God sees you, or to see yourself as the world sees you.

Ask God to continue to open your spiritual eyes as you serve in His kingdom.

Lord Jesus, allow Your Holy Spirit to rise up in me, teaching me Your truth and filling me with Your love, peace, and hope. Help me to choose Your way of living. Open my eyes to see my life from Your perspective.

GOD IS ABLE

And God is able to bless you abundantly, so that in all things at all times, having all that you need, you will abound in every good work.
2 CORINTHIANS 9:8 NIV

It has been said that "sometimes God doesn't always deliver you *from*; sometimes He delivers you *through*, and He delivers you *in*."

Do you believe God is able to be and do and provide everything you need? Press into this thought in prayer. Bring your thoughts, feelings, and doubts to God. He can handle your honesty. Allow Him access to align your thoughts and feelings with His truth. What does He want you to know?

Let this scripture from Jude 24–25 (NIV) be your encouragement today: "To him who is able to keep you from stumbling and to present you before his glorious presence without fault and with great joy—to the only God our Savior be glory, majesty, power and authority, through Jesus Christ our Lord, before all ages, now and forevermore! Amen."

God, I need You to strengthen my faith. I want to believe You are able. Help my unbelief.

BLESSINGS FROM GOD

Every good thing given and every perfect gift is from above; it comes down from the Father of lights [the Creator and Sustainer of the heavens], in whom there is no variation [no rising or setting] or shadow cast by His turning [for He is perfect and never changes].

JAMES 1:17 AMP

God is perfect. His ways are perfect. His gifts are perfect. And He wants to bless you.

John 1:16 (NLV) says, "From Him Who has so much we have all received loving-favor, one loving-favor after another." The Amplified Bible says it this way: "For out of His fullness [the superabundance of His grace and truth] we have all received grace upon grace [spiritual blessing upon spiritual blessing, favor upon favor, and gift heaped upon gift]."

When you ask God to give you spiritual eyes and a heart of thankfulness, you can begin to see even hardships as gifts from God. He knows what He's doing. He's good at His job. He loves you and wants the best for you.

Lord, I know Your plan is to make everything right again. I trust You with my heart. Thank You for Your eternal blessings.

A CALL TO WORSHIP

Happy are those who hear the joyful call to worship, for they will walk in the light of your presence, Lord. They rejoice all day long in your wonderful reputation. They exult in your righteousness.

Psalm 89:15–16 NLT

Traditionally, Jewish people pray three times a day. In Bible times, a special horn called a shofar was blown at the start of a new prayer week, as well as during special religious festivals, as a call to prayer and repentance. God's people had special rhythms in place to remind them to worship, pray, and repent. The Psalms tell us that those who rejoice in the reminder to go to God in worship, prayer, and repentance are blessed.

Because of Jesus, you are free. You are not bound by specific religious practices anymore. Our righteousness is in Christ alone. But in this distracted world we live in, daily rhythms of prayer and worship can be a huge blessing to us that we can miss if we're not intentional.

What kind of worship rhythm can you include in your daily walk with God?

Lord, I'm happy to praise You. I want more of You in my life.

A GOD OF BLESSING

"Blessed is the one who trusts in the Lord, whose confidence is in him. They will be like a tree planted by the water that sends out its roots by the stream. It does not fear when heat comes; its leaves are always green. It has no worries in a year of drought and never fails to bear fruit."

Jeremiah 17:7–8 NIV

God is the wisest and most loving Father. With a heart of thankfulness, read through these timeless and eternal truths:

- "How abundant are the good things that you have stored up for those who fear you, that you bestow in the sight of all, on those who take refuge in you" (Psalm 31:19 NIV).
- "Open your mouth and taste, open your eyes and see—how good God is. Blessed are you who run to him" (Psalm 34:8 MSG).
- "God blesses us, and all the ends of the earth shall fear Him [with awe-inspired reverence and submissive wonder]" (Psalm 67:7 AMP).

Thank You for Your abundant blessings, Lord. Even in difficult times, I see Your hand at work and Your plan to redeem in place.

PSALM 23

The Lord *is my shepherd, I lack nothing. He makes me lie down in green pastures, he leads me beside quiet waters, he refreshes my soul. He guides me along the right paths for his name's sake.*

Psalm 23:1–3 niv

The Twenty-Third Psalm is recited frequently, especially at funerals. You may already know it by heart in the King James Version. But have you ever stopped to picture this scripture in your mind? The Bible is full of beautiful imagery. Close your eyes in prayer and think of it this way: "The Eternal is my shepherd, He cares for me always. He provides me rest in rich, green fields beside streams of refreshing water. He soothes my fears; He makes me whole again, steering me off worn, hard paths to roads where truth and righteousness echo His name" (Psalm 23:1–3 voice).

Wouldn't you like to get off worn, hard paths and walk on good roads with Jesus? Take His hand. He's always ready to walk with you.

Lord, You are my good shepherd. Lead me and I will follow.

AT HOME

Jesus replied, "Anyone who loves me will obey my teaching. My Father will love them, and we will come to them and make our home with them."
John 14:23 NIV

The Christian life is not about doing more and being better. That's what empty religion requires of a person. It's a heavy responsibility that drags people into a futile shame cycle. That is not what Jesus came to do! He came to bring an abundant life of joy, peace, adventure, and purpose in everything. . .even in the pain.

Religion without the power of God's Spirit alive and at work in you will only bring death. It forces you to keep digging—to keep working to the point of exhaustion. In contrast, Jesus is calling you into life and grace.

Jesus is drawing you ever closer to Himself. He doesn't burden you with heavy weights. To paraphrase Pastor Robert Gelinas of Colorado Community Church: "Jesus says, Abide in Me. Live in Me. Let Me be your home. Be comfortable. Kick off your shoes. Be at home in Me."

Jesus, come and make my heart Your home.

ATTITUDE

"Anyone who chooses to do the will of God will find out whether my teaching comes from God or whether I speak on my own."
JOHN 7:17 NIV

God loves us so much that He sent His only Son to take away our sins and set us free. And He gave us the choice to believe and follow Him, or not. We get to choose if we will respond to problems with faith. We get to choose our attitude.

And our attitude impacts so many things in our lives. Attitudes are so powerful they can either build up or destroy businesses, churches, and homes. The good news is that we get to choose our attitude every single day. When we fully embrace this truth, we accept that the past is in the past. We quit trying to change people and instead focus on ourselves and what we can control. So today, choose an attitude of love, joy, hope, humility. Let God take care of the rest!

Lord, help me choose a thankful attitude.

FROM DARKNESS TO LIGHT

Again Jesus spoke to them, saying, "I am the light of the world. Whoever follows me will not walk in darkness, but will have the light of life."

JOHN 8:12 ESV

The Voice Bible puts it this way: "I am the light that shines through the cosmos; if you walk with Me, you will thrive in the nourishing light that gives life and will not know darkness."

Most of us have experienced pain and betrayal in this life. Some more than most. Those who've faced utter darkness and untold evils either succumb to the great deceiver or reach out for the light. Those are the only two choices at that point. Either people become convinced there is no real hope, or they allow Jesus to be their only hope. Either He's real and everything the Bible says is true. . .or He's not.

Maybe you've firmly decided these things in your life, but likely there is someone in your world who hasn't and is desperate for hope. Pray for them daily and share God's love and light as He leads you.

Lord, thank You for Your nourishing light in my life. Give me eyes to see others who need Your light too.

TILL IT OVERFLOWS

"The thief comes only in order to steal and kill and destroy. I came that they may have and enjoy life, and have it in abundance [to the full, till it overflows]."
JOHN 10:10 AMP

American missionary A. W. Tozer said, "An infinite God can give all of Himself to each of His children. He does not distribute Himself that each may have a part, but to each one He gives all of Himself as fully as if there were no others."

Psalm 139 reminds us that God knows us intimately. He knows things about us that no one else could know and things about us that we don't even know yet ourselves.

He came to give you an abundant life, starting the day you say "Yes" to Jesus. He wants to heal your heart in all the broken places, tell you the truth about who you are, and live life with you in each moment.

Life will never be easy, but it will always be full of His blessing and adventure as you live life in His presence.

I want this abundant life that You offer me, Jesus.
Fill me with Your life until it overflows.

BLESSING OTHERS THROUGH PRAYER

For this reason, since the day we heard about you, we have not stopped praying for you. We continually ask God to fill you with the knowledge of his will through all the wisdom and understanding that the Spirit gives, so that you may live a life worthy of the Lord and please him in every way: bearing fruit in every good work, growing in the knowledge of God, being strengthened with all power according to his glorious might so that you may have great endurance and patience, and giving joyful thanks to the Father, who has qualified you to share in the inheritance of his holy people in the kingdom of light.

COLOSSIANS 1:9–12 NIV

The Bible tells us that our prayers are powerful in a mysterious way. Heavenly assignments are given when we go to God in prayer. Believe it: Your prayers matter and they make a difference.

Spend extra time in prayer today for the people in your life. Write down your requests and date them. Keep watch and pray. Wait and see what God will do.

Lord, I trust that You hear my prayers and work on my behalf.

A DAILY BLESSING

Enter his gates with thanksgiving; go into his courts with praise. Give thanks to him and praise his name. For the LORD is good. His unfailing love continues forever, and his faithfulness continues to each generation.

PSALM 100:4–5 NLT

Many people wake up tired, grumpy, and stiff. But God's people have a hope that goes beyond our feelings. Consider choosing joy and blessing when you wake. Try coming up with an early morning prayer that becomes your daily blessing. Maybe something like this:

> *I come into Your presence with praise. May I know that You, Lord God, are mighty, powerful, and gracious. May I see You as my hope and deliverer today. Pour out Your love into my life so that it overflows to others. Amen.*

Take your thoughts captive today and set them on heavenly things. Attitude is everything. And you always have a choice in that.

Thank You, Lord, for Your blessing in my life. I choose to set my mind and heart on You. I commit my thoughts and actions to You today.

WHY PEOPLE DO THE THINGS THEY DO

Let all bitterness and wrath and anger and clamor and slander be put away from you, along with all malice. Be kind to one another, tenderhearted, forgiving one another, as God in Christ forgave you.

Ephesians 4:31–32 esv

What are some of the strangest, most outlandish things you've witnessed people doing? Whether you believe it or not, the truth is that many times there is some logic behind even the craziest human actions. Think about it. . . .

People have legitimate longings that they are not allowing God to meet, so they go about trying to get these needs met on their own. This comes out as all kinds of crazy. You probably run into these people several times a day. Ask God to give you compassion for them. They are searching and haven't found what they need yet. A gracious heart and a kind word can help (compassion is something they probably haven't experienced much in their lives), but guard against getting sucked in by their behavior.

Lord Jesus, please give me Your heart for others. Help me show love and care in healthy ways.

MANY HAPPY DAYS

For the Scriptures say, "If you want to enjoy life and see many happy days, keep your tongue from speaking evil and your lips from telling lies. Turn away from evil and do good. Search for peace, and work to maintain it. The eyes of the LORD watch over those who do right, and his ears are open to their prayers. But the LORD turns his face against those who do evil."

1 PETER 3:10–12 NLT

This little nugget of truth for life is tucked away in the book of 1 Peter, and it's better than your daily vitamin. Want to see happy days? Follow God's plan for your life!

Verse 11 in the Amplified Bible explains it this way: "He must turn away from wickedness and do what is right. He must search for peace [with God, with self, with others] and pursue it eagerly [actively—not merely desiring it]."

You are righteous in Christ alone. Because you are His child, God's eyes are on you. His ears hear you. He will lead you into all truth. But His face is against those who do evil.

My happiness is found in You, Lord. Help me follow Your ways.

ALL DAY LONG

Show me your ways, LORD, teach me your paths. Guide me in your truth and teach me, for you are God my Savior, and my hope is in you all day long.

PSALM 25:4–5 NIV

God speaks so clearly when you are listening and pressing into Him, giving Him your heart and your time, and seeking His face before your own desires. Prayerfully consider these scriptures:

- "He refreshes my soul. He guides me along the right paths for his name's sake" (Psalm 23:3 NIV).
- "Teach me your way, LORD; lead me in a straight path. . . . I remain confident of this: I will see the goodness of the LORD in the land of the living. Wait for the LORD; be strong and take heart and wait for the LORD" (Psalm 27:11, 13–14 NIV).
- "You will show me the way of life. Being with You is to be full of joy. In Your right hand there is happiness forever" (Psalm 16:11 NLV).

Lord, I'm convinced that You lovingly guide me on the path of life. I want to know and follow Your voice. My hope is in You all day long.

AT THE CROSSROADS

"Because of the tender mercy of our God, by which the rising sun will come to us from heaven to shine on those living in darkness and in the shadow of death, to guide our feet into the path of peace."

LUKE 1:78–79 NIV

Have you ever been at a major crossroads in life? One where the decision you make will affect the rest of your life and perhaps that of your family? God has wisdom for you in those places. You will find the answer to all of your questions in Christ.

"This is what the LORD says: 'Stand at the crossroads and look; ask for the ancient paths, ask where the good way is, and walk in it, and you will find rest for your souls'" (Jeremiah 6:16 NIV).

In those places of major decision-making, lean heavily on Christ. He promises to guide your feet, step by step, into paths of peace. Trust Him.

Thank You, Jesus! For seeing me. For hearing my heart. For caring about what concerns me. Please lead me into Your peace as I trust in You.

CREATIVE PROBLEM-SOLVING

When the three hundred trumpets sounded,
the LORD caused the men throughout the camp
to turn on each other with their swords.
JUDGES 7:22 NIV

Are you familiar with the story of Gideon? Gideon was a farmer whom God unexpectedly chose to use in a fascinating way to save His people. With only three hundred men against the much larger Midianite army of thousands, Gideon snuck into the enemy's camp, and God caused the enemy army to turn on each other so that they fought amongst themselves! Gideon's men didn't have to do a thing but blow their trumpets and smash some jars! Gideon's army watched as God won the battle, reminding us all that our victory doesn't come from our own strength.

God is all-powerful and the source of all creativity. His ways are not your ways. When you are trying to solve a problem, go to Him first. Trust Him. When you are up against a seemingly impossible situation, rely on His faithfulness and His ability to come through for you in ways you never thought possible.

Lord God, You are the Mighty One. Help me trust Your ability to fight any battle.

GOD'S DECREE

"No weapon forged against you will prevail, and you will refute every tongue that accuses you. This is the heritage of the servants of the LORD, and this is their vindication from me," declares the LORD.

ISAIAH 54:17 NIV

The Message says it this way: "'No weapon that can hurt you has ever been forged. Any accuser who takes you to court will be dismissed as a liar. This is what GOD's servants can expect. I'll see to it that everything works out for the best.' GOD's Decree."

Life is hard. Everyone comes under a period of attack from the outside world. Jesus wants you to trust Him in times like these. He offers you a beautiful heritage as His beloved child. You are not alone. God is working out everything for your good and His glory as you trust Him. Solid faith is forged in the fires of life. But just as God was with Shadrach, Meshach, and Abednego, He is with you. As you find your refuge in Him, He will keep you from getting burned.

Lord God, I come to You in this trial.
Help me trust in Your faithfulness.

JOY AND RIGHTEOUSNESS

I am overwhelmed with joy in the LORD my God! For he has dressed me with the clothing of salvation and draped me in a robe of righteousness. I am like a bridegroom dressed for his wedding or a bride with her jewels.

ISAIAH 61:10 NLT

If you've ever beat yourself up for past mistakes, this message is for you. If you struggle with shame over your past, this message is for you. Come to Jesus.

Picture this. As you come to Him, He gently removes your guilt and wipes away the tears and shame of your past. He paid for it all on the cross. He lifts your head. He drapes you in righteousness and makes you whole and holy. Ephesians 1:4 (ESV) says, "He chose us in him before the foundation of the world, that we should be holy and blameless before him."

If you're feeling empty, you can be replenished with this truth: Christ fills everything in every way (Ephesians 1:23). Joy is yours as you stand in the truth of His righteousness wrapped around you.

Fill me with joy, Jesus, as You remove my shame and wrap me in Your righteousness!

HOPE AND POWER

I pray that the eyes of your heart may be enlightened in order that you may know the hope to which he has called you, the riches of his glorious inheritance in his holy people, and his incomparably great power for us who believe.

EPHESIANS 1:18–19 NIV

As a follower of Christ, you have incomparably great power. It's yours! It's alive in you!

What kind of power? Ephesians 1:19–21 (NIV) explains: "That power is the same as the mighty strength he exerted when he raised Christ from the dead and seated him at his right hand in the heavenly realms, far above all rule and authority, power and dominion, and every name that is invoked, not only in the present age but also in the one to come."

Yes, the same power that raised Christ from the dead is what is alive and at work in you! Right now and for all eternity. Jesus has called you to this great hope. Believe it. Walk in it.

Lord, thank You for the great hope You've given me. Help me walk each day in Your truth and power.

OUR DEFEATED FOE

But let us who live in the light be clearheaded, protected by the armor of faith and love, and wearing as our helmet the confidence of our salvation.
1 THESSALONIANS 5:8 NLT

The Bible tells us that we have an enemy. He is known as the father of lies (John 8:44), the accuser who makes us feel bad about ourselves (Revelation 12:10), and the ruler of darkness (Ephesians 6:12). But here's the really important thing you need to know: Because of Jesus, Satan doesn't have any power over you (Colossians 2:15)! Even though the enemy knows he has been defeated, he is still trying his best to get into your head and discourage you so much that you won't be able to live for Jesus. That's why Jesus wants you to stay alert and put on your armor: "Be strong with the Lord's strength. Put on the things God gives you to fight with. Then you will not fall into the traps of the devil" (Ephesians 6:10–11 NLV).

Lord, thank You for giving me armor to protect myself against the enemy. I will be strong in Your strength.

HE TAKES OUR HAND

"I am the Lord. I have called you to be right and good. I will hold you by the hand and watch over you. And I will give you as an agreement to the people, as a light to the nations."

ISAIAH 42:6 NLV

God has called His people to righteousness and holiness. But He is a good, good Father. He doesn't just give us an impossible task and sit back to watch us fail. An unwise parent will tell a young child to clean their room and leave them to it. But a loving and wise parent will first show the child what is expected of them and help them to finish the task well.

God Himself comes to live inside us, giving us the power to live life through Him. He takes our hand. We could never be righteous on our own, so He takes up residence in our hearts and floods us with light and life and love.

Lord Jesus, I'm so grateful that I don't have to figure life out on my own. I'm holding tightly to Your hand.

YOUR HEART IS FREE

But whenever anyone turns to the Lord, the veil is taken away. Now the Lord is the Spirit, and where the Spirit of the Lord is, there is freedom. And we all, who with unveiled faces contemplate the Lord's glory, are being transformed into his image with ever-increasing glory, which comes from the Lord, who is the Spirit.

2 CORINTHIANS 3:16–18 NIV

As we turn to Christ, we are being transformed into His image and our hearts become free. The New Life Version says, "The heart is free where the Spirit of the Lord is" (2 Corinthians 3:17).

What do you need Jesus to free in you today? Are you finding yourself stuck in certain areas of your life? Are your relationships suffering in ways that you can't fix? Bring them to Jesus. Lift them up to His throne and ask for His truth and His freedom. Some things aren't yours to fix. Laying these things down before Jesus can set your heart free.

Jesus, I feel burdened in certain relationships and areas of my life that I can't seem to fix. Please give me wisdom as I lay them at Your feet. Free my heart as I worship You.

AT THE CROSS

The message of the cross is foolish to those who are headed for destruction! But we who are being saved know it is the very power of God.

1 Corinthians 1:18 NLT

"Saint Patrick's Breastplate" is a prayer from around the eleventh century. Let this excerpt be your fervent prayer today:

Christ with me, Christ before me,
Christ behind me, Christ in me,
Christ beneath me, Christ above me,
Christ on my right, Christ on my left. . .
Christ in the heart of every man who thinks of me,
Christ in the mouth of everyone who speaks of me,
Christ in every eye that sees me,
Christ in every ear that hears me.

Because you are God's child, the cross of Christ comes between you and all mankind. Nothing but the blood of Jesus and the love of Jesus can come between you and all things and people now unless you choose to place your faith in something other than the cross of Christ.

Jesus, I put all my faith in You alone. I am protected and surrounded by the truth of who You are.

OUT OF DARKNESS

He brought them out of darkness, the utter darkness, and broke away their chains.
PSALM 107:14 NIV

Broken people often wall themselves off from pain so they won't be hurt again. At first, this is an innate protective mechanism. But as time goes on and healing goes unpursued, these walls built for protection become prisons instead. The problem with building walls is that while pain might not get in, love and light can't get in either.

Bring your wounded heart to Jesus. Let Him be Your protector and defender. As He heals your heart, you will begin to believe and understand this truth: "You are a chosen people, a royal priesthood, a holy nation, God's special possession, that you may declare the praises of him who called you out of darkness into his wonderful light" (1 Peter 2:9 NIV).

Jesus, help me to receive Your healing light in my life. I bring You my broken heart. Please do what only You can do.

THE INVITATION

Search me [thoroughly], O God, and know my heart; test me and know my anxious thoughts; and see if there is any wicked or hurtful way in me, and lead me in the everlasting way.
PSALM 139:23–24 AMP

God is relentless in His pursuit of you. To paraphrase a prayer from the *Wild at Heart* podcast: He will stop at nothing to continue opening the door and inviting you home. He wants access to all of you. He's waiting for your "yes". . .to be made whole and holy. He wants to unite your heart with His heart. He wants to break every limit you've placed on His power. He wants to restore your soul.

Where do you need God to shine His light, exposing every place in you that has yet to come home to Him? Bring these areas to Jesus in prayer.

Search me, Lord God. Shine Your light into my heart. Bring to the surface anything that needs to be cleaned out and dealt with. Forgive me for limiting Your power in my life. I invite You in. Restore my soul.

FLIP THE SWITCH

Dear brothers and sisters, when troubles of any kind come your way, consider it an opportunity for great joy. For you know that when your faith is tested, your endurance has a chance to grow.

JAMES 1:2–3 NLT

When trouble comes, we have two basic choices: We can freak out. Or we can trust. Remember that God is a good Father. When we choose to trust in His love and faithfulness, He prepares us for the hard times with help and resources and His very presence. When we choose to freak out instead, we are basically telling God we don't believe He can help in this particular situation: "Sorry, God, but the only way I can get through this is to power through alone. Thanks but no thanks."

Which response is going to bring about God's blessing? "Lord, I believe; help my unbelief!" is a very valid prayer. If you're struggling with faith, bring your doubts to Jesus. Repent and ask Him to fill you with greater trust.

Choose to flip the switch and begin seeing problems as opportunities to increase your faith muscles.

Jesus, I confess my lack of faith when it comes to problems. Please increase my faith!

POUR OUT YOUR HEART

Hope deferred makes the heart sick,
but a longing fulfilled is a tree of life.
PROVERBS 13:12 NIV

The story of Hannah in 1 Samuel 1–2 is one of great hope. We see her depressed and desperate at the beginning of the story. She is bullied and made fun of because she has no children. She hates going to the temple because of all the verbal abuse she endures there. She's so sick she can't eat.

But then she begins pouring her heart out to God. She lets loose with God, so much so that the priest thinks she's drunk! But as she brings all of her feelings to the surface with God, He gives her great hope. She goes away radiant, and God answers her prayers for a child.

Can you relate to Hannah? Bring your tears to God and let Him give you hope. Take courage from Psalm 62:8 (NLT): "O my people, trust in him at all times. Pour out your heart to him, for God is our refuge."

God, I bring You all my thoughts and feelings.
I need Your help and Your hope.

THOUGHTS MATTER

Finally, brothers and sisters, whatever is true, whatever is noble, whatever is right, whatever is pure, whatever is lovely, whatever is admirable— if anything is excellent or praiseworthy—think about such things.

PHILIPPIANS 4:8 NIV

Our thoughts are very important to God. He wants our thinking to line up with His truth. As a follower of Jesus, you have been given new life. This new life changes everything, including your thought patterns.

Second Corinthians 5:17 (NLT) says, "This means that anyone who belongs to Christ has become a new person. The old life is gone; a new life has begun!" If you're struggling with the same old thinking, you have authority and power through Christ to command any ungodly thoughts to leave in the name of Jesus. Say the name of Jesus out loud the next time you find your mind wandering!

Jesus, I want my thoughts to align with Your truth. Make my mind brand-new.

Remaining in Christ

"I am the vine; you are the branches. If you remain in me and I in you, you will bear much fruit; apart from me you can do nothing."
John 15:5 niv

Remaining in Christ, abiding in Him, is the only way to live out the Christian life with power and victory. If you've accepted Jesus Christ as your Savior, then certain strength is yours (Isaiah 41:10). Why? Because it comes from the power of the Holy Spirit alive inside of you. Either we believe this as Christians. . . or what is the point? In John 16:7 (esv) Jesus says, "Nevertheless, I tell you the truth: it is to your advantage that I go away, for if I do not go away, the Helper will not come to you. But if I go, I will send him to you."

With God's Spirit alive in us, we have the power to remain close to Jesus, living out His very life and purpose for us forever.

Spirit of God, fill me to the brim with Your love and power. I need Your help every moment to live a new and different life.

GOD'S PEOPLE

The Lord *gives strength to his people;*
the Lord *blesses his people with peace.*
Psalm 29:11 NIV

When you become a child of God, you are instantly granted heavenly privileges. Look them up, write them down, and start believing them today:

- I am free and clean in the blood of Christ (Galatians 5:1; 1 John 1:7).
- He has rescued me from darkness and brought me into His kingdom (Colossians 1:13).
- I have direct access to God (Ephesians 2:18).
- I am a precious child of the Father (Isaiah 43:6–7; John 1:12; Galatians 3:26).
- I am a friend of Christ (John 15:15).
- Nothing can separate me from God's love (Romans 8:38–39).
- God is for me, not against me (Romans 8:31).
- He delights in me (Psalm 149:4).
- I am God's temple (1 Corinthians 3:16).
- I am chosen by God (Colossians 3:12).

Thank You, Jesus!

ACCEPTING THE TRUTH

For God gave us a spirit not of fear but of power and love and self-control.
2 TIMOTHY 1:7 ESV

The Passion Translation says it this way: "For God will never give you the spirit of fear, but the Holy Spirit who gives you mighty power, love, and self-control."

If you are experiencing discouragement, defeat, fear, or depression, you can know for sure that those feelings didn't come from God. It's time to align your thinking with God's Word. And His Word says that perfect love casts out fear (1 John 4:18). The Spirit who is alive in you is full of power, love, soundness of mind, and abilities beyond your own power and understanding. Search out these truths from God's Word. Ask Him to show you what is real and what is true. Then take every thought captive (2 Corinthians 10:5), rejecting lies about God, yourself, and others and instead accepting God's truth.

Jesus, I need strength from Your Spirit to come against these lies. In Your powerful name and perfect love, I cast out any fear or discouragement that is coming against me.

WHO YOU REALLY ARE

Beloved, let us love one another, for love is from God, and whoever loves has been born of God and knows God.
1 JOHN 4:7 ESV

God calls you beloved. Is that how you see yourself? If you look up the word *beloved* in a dictionary or thesaurus, you can learn more about God's heart for you. As His beloved, you are dear, esteemed, His favorite, prized, respected, treasured, liked. We know God's Word tells us that He loves us, but did you know that God likes you too?

Do these words line up with how you view yourself? Go through each synonym of *beloved* again and thank God for loving you, for respecting you, for liking you, and so on. If you struggle with seeing yourself this way, ask God to remove any walls you've built around your heart. Ask Him to remove the blinders so you can see yourself the way He sees you.

Jesus, I'm so amazed at how You see me. Forgive me for when I put myself down and struggle with self-image. Please give me spiritual eyes to see myself the way You do.

IN THE MORNING WHEN I RISE

For you know that it was not with perishable things such as silver or gold that you were redeemed from the empty way of life handed down to you from your ancestors, but with the precious blood of Christ, a lamb without blemish or defect.

1 PETER 1:18–19 NIV

Your morning routine has a way of setting up your whole day. Waking up late and rushing out the door tends to set a person up for a rough day. But planning ahead, even if doing so takes just a few extra minutes, can make all the difference in the outcome of your day.

How can you wake up with God's truth on your heart? Start with thanksgiving for a new day as soon as your eyes are open (or maybe after that first fresh cup of magical beans!). Maybe leave a note right by your coffeemaker that says, "I am His; He is mine." Meditate on that thought as you get dressed and prepare for your day.

Jesus, please help me get into a new morning groove, with my mind set on You.

CHOSEN AND BROUGHT NEAR

Blessed is the one whom You choose and bring near to dwell in Your courts. We will be filled with the goodness of Your house, Your holy temple.

Psalm 65:4 AMP

The truth of God's Word for us is mind-boggling when you really stop and think about it. You've been chosen by God (1 Peter 2:9) and He brings you close to Him. He wants a deep and personal relationship with you (Psalm 139). You are His beloved daughter and He delights in you (Zephaniah 3:17). He fills you with His goodness.

Many of God's children struggle with self-image and insecurity. If you're not one of them, fantastic! But there are probably quite a few women in your life who do. This message is for you and for them. Ask Jesus to help you believe His Word is all true, to your very core. Then ask God what He wants you to do with this message. Can you share it with other women who are struggling?

Jesus, I want to share Your amazing truth with other women. Please point me in the right direction. Show me how I can help others lift their heads to You.

CONFESSION

So let God work his will in you. Yell a loud no to the Devil and watch him make himself scarce. Say a quiet yes to God and he'll be there in no time. Quit dabbling in sin. Purify your inner life. Quit playing the field. Hit bottom, and cry your eyes out. The fun and games are over. Get serious, really serious. Get down on your knees before the Master; it's the only way you'll get on your feet.

JAMES 4:7–10 MSG

God wants you on your feet. Loving Him, being loved, and sharing that love with others. It's hard to do that when you're bogged down with the same old sins. Time to get real. Get alone with God and allow Him to bring anything unholy to the surface. He wants to wash you clean. Let Him work His will in you. Yell that loud "No!" to the devil, in Jesus' name. And say "Yes!" to Jesus as He works in your heart.

Jesus, I bring all of myself to You, today. I confess my failings and my hidden sins. Wash me clean in Your blood. I don't want to take Your death for granted anymore.

EVERY THOUGHT MATTERS

Don't copy the behavior and customs of this world, but let God transform you into a new person by changing the way you think. Then you will learn to know God's will for you, which is good and pleasing and perfect.

ROMANS 12:2 NLT

God cares about your thoughts. And the good news is that our thoughts can be directed toward healthy, positive ideas and away from hurtful, negative patterns of thinking.

As believers, we want to align our thoughts with the truth of God's Word. We continue to "take captive every thought to make it obedient to Christ" (2 Corinthians 10:5 NIV).

God has so much wisdom to share with us about how to think and how to relate to others. He doesn't want us to be intimidated by toxic people or our own wrong thinking. Every thought matters.

Lord, highlight any wrong thinking in me.
Show me how to align my thoughts with Yours.

NATURE IS HEALING

Let the fields and their crops burst out with joy!
Let the trees of the forest sing for joy.
PSALM 96:12 NLT

Research has shown in the past that roughly 90 percent of people spend twenty-two hours or more inside every day. Not surprisingly, so much time indoors contributes to very poor health statistics. God created mankind to enjoy His creation. He intended for nature to help heal our bodies. Our cortisol levels lower when we take a walk. Oxygen released from trees helps our lungs and cells do their jobs as we inhale. Our white blood cells increase. Studies have shown that nature walks improve our emotional state, reducing anger and stress. Even your blood pressure is positively affected.

Make time to get out in God's creation. Thank Him for the healing attributes He planned all around you. Enjoy His presence in each season. As Isaiah 55:12 (ESV) says, "You shall go out in joy and be led forth in peace; the mountains and the hills before you shall break forth into singing, and all the trees of the field shall clap their hands." Will you join them in praise?

Thank You, Lord God, for Your beautiful creation and its purposes.

WHEN YOU'VE LOST YOUR JOY

I pray that God, the source of hope, will fill you completely with joy and peace because you trust in him. Then you will overflow with confident hope through the power of the Holy Spirit.

Romans 15:13 NLT

Life is hard. We lose loved ones. We experience pain and betrayal. Trauma occurs, and we have little explanation for it. Our happiness and joy get buried underneath our survival instincts. To say that Jesus is our only hope is no cliché. When we hit rock bottom, either everything Jesus says about Himself is true, or there really is no hope at all.

Where did laughter go? Will joy ever return?

Romans 15:13 tells us we can have joy and peace only by the power of His Spirit alive within us. We don't have to be fake and muster up happiness in our own strength.

As you submit yourself to God's healing process in your heart and bring all of your pain to the surface for Him to sift through. . .you will find that His power causes hope and joy to bubble back up within you.

Jesus, You alone are my source of hope. I trust You to bring back my joy as You heal my heart.

CULTIVATING JOY

A happy heart is good medicine and a joyful mind causes healing, but a broken spirit dries up the bones.

PROVERBS 17:22 AMP

Aren't you glad that God can give us joy in abundance? It is a fruit of the Spirit that needs cultivated by the master gardener Himself.

Jesus invites you to come to Him with everything. The choice is yours. Will you give Him full access to the garden of your heart? Allow Him to pull weeds and tend to your needs. Let Him refresh you with His living water. Let Him plant seeds of joy, even if you feel like you don't deserve it or you're just not ready. Trust the Master and His timing.

As you give Him permission to heal your hurts and heartaches, He supernaturally gives you rest and peace. And as you linger in His very presence, He fills you with His joy that brings healing (Psalm 16:11).

Jesus, I do want Your healing touch in my life. I submit to Your plan to pull out the weeds and begin tending to my heart.

LETTING GO MAKES ROOM FOR JOY

"Do not remember the former things, or ponder the things of the past. Listen carefully, I am about to do a new thing, now it will spring forth; will you not be aware of it? I will even put a road in the wilderness, rivers in the desert."

ISAIAH 43:18–19 AMP

Like all of us, you probably have some things in your past you'd really like to forget. But heated conversations and failures often replay themselves in your mind, stealing your focus. And stealing your joy.

Jesus doesn't want you to keep carrying those burdens around. You can't fix everything, and you certainly can't fix other people. But you can fix your mind on Christ!

As Philippians 3:13–14 (NIV) reminds us: "Forgetting what is behind and straining toward what is ahead, I press on toward the goal to win the prize for which God has called me heavenward in Christ Jesus."

Jesus, please help me let go of past failures that steal my joy. I choose to fix my mind on You.

THE WAYS OF CHRIST

Who ever knows what you're thinking and planning except you yourself? The same with God—except that he not only knows what he's thinking, but he lets us in on it.
1 CORINTHIANS 2:11–12 MSG

The New Living Translation says it this way: "And we have received God's Spirit (not the world's spirit), so we can know the wonderful things God has freely given us."

Why is this so extremely important? Because if we don't have God's Spirit alive in us, we can't possibly know or follow the ways of Christ. But because we do. . .we can!

Ask God to help you begin to see life as a wonderful and epic adventure. Trouble may come, but you know where your power comes from too. You wouldn't want to watch a movie without any suspense or adventure at all in it, would you? It would be boring. Life needs challenges that strengthen our faith.

Lord, open my eyes to see Your ways of adventure and challenge as good things. Thank You for Your Spirit, who teaches me Your ways on this journey.

SHAPED BY GOD'S LIFE

So roll up your sleeves, get your head in the game, be totally ready to receive the gift that's coming when Jesus arrives. Don't lazily slip back into those old grooves of evil, doing just what you feel like doing. You didn't know any better then; you do now. As obedient children, let yourselves be pulled into a way of life shaped by God's life, a life energetic and blazing with holiness. God said, "I am holy; you be holy."

1 Peter 1:13–16 MSG

The Christian life is not a set of rules you must follow to please God. . .that's religion. The difference in following Jesus is that His Spirit is alive in you. That's where the power comes from to live the Christian life! You don't have to muster strength on your own to accomplish the impossible. It's all about surrendering your heart, mind, and will to the Holy One. His power alone is what enables you to live for Him!

Allow Jesus to shape your life the way He wants to. You'll find an abundant life blazing with holiness.

Jesus, thank You for Your work in me!

AS ALIVE AS CHRIST

When God lives and breathes in you (and he does, as surely as he did in Jesus), you are delivered from that dead life. With his Spirit living in you, your body will be as alive as Christ's!

ROMANS 8:11 MSG

Imagine what your life would be like if you believed this truth every moment of every day: God Himself is living and breathing in you! That's exactly what the Bible tells us.

Many Christians don't live like they believe this truth at all. They think we're just meant to endure this difficult life until we get to heaven. But the truth is that Jesus lived, died, and rose again to save us from our sins so we could be restored to God. He heals. He delivers. He makes all things new. He desires an intimate relationship with us—with me and you!—which means so much more than "religion."

If the Christian life you're experiencing doesn't match the abundant life that God's Word promises, press in. Take a deeper look.

Spirit of Christ, come alive in me!

LOVE, NOT JUDGMENT

Jesus knew what they were thinking. He said, "Why do you think bad thoughts in your hearts?"

MATTHEW 9:4 NLV

Whether we realize it or not, we are often judging relentlessly throughout each day: What we like, what we don't, whether that outfit looks cute on her or not, whether your hair looks good or hers looks bad. . .we are constantly judging something or someone, including ourselves.

God does give you discernment, which is not the same as judgment but rather is an internal warning system to help alert you when something is off or you are in danger. You can be alert to unsafe feelings when you're around other people and at the same time filter those feelings through the love of Jesus, asking Him for wisdom to love others while keeping healthy boundaries.

Ask God to help you start paying attention to your judgmental thoughts and to help you overcome them. You'll find the weight of the world slipping off your shoulders as you begin to love others instead of judging them.

God, please forgive me for my constant judging. Help me see myself and others through eyes of love.

CHOSEN, HOLY, AND DEARLY LOVED

Therefore, as God's chosen people, holy and dearly loved, clothe yourselves with compassion, kindness, humility, gentleness and patience.
COLOSSIANS 3:12 NIV

Acts 10:34 tells us that God is no respecter of persons. Other versions say that God doesn't show favoritism. God values you just as much as all the famous Christians down through history and all the heroes from the Bible. No one Christian is better or more valuable in God's kingdom than you are.

You are an important part of the body of Christ. You are a dearly loved child of God, and everything you do has value and purpose in His kingdom. Not because of anything you have done or ever could do on your own. . .but simply because you're God's beloved daughter. God's chosen one. Holy and blameless because of Jesus.

As you come to know your true value in God's eyes, He gives you the ability to treat people compassionately, with kindness and respect.

Lord, I believe what You say is true. Thank You for making me a valued part of Your body. Help me to treat others with kindness as I further Your kingdom.

FREEDOM IN CHRIST

"So if the Son sets you free, you are truly free."
JOHN 8:36 NLT

"Jesus paid it all; all to Him I owe." You've heard the old hymn. But here's the thing—Jesus says you owe Him nothing! He says there are no charges against you. You're free to go. He paid it all for you. The Bible says that He casts your sins into the depths of the sea and remembers them no more (Micah 7:19).

Freedom in Christ means you don't have to carry around a heavy load of guilt and shame. He wants you to walk in your freedom. He paid dearly for it. Jesus won't load you up with rules and guilt. That's religion. . .not Jesus. Dependence on Jesus brings rest and freedom (Matthew 11:28–30).

You are *free*! Accept it. Believe it. Walk in that truth. If you are struggling in this area, bring these thoughts to Jesus. Ask Him to highlight anything in you that might be preventing you from believing this truth from His Word.

Jesus, help me to believe the truth that I am free. I'm so thankful for the price you paid for that freedom.

TRUE REST

"Come to me, all you who are weary and burdened, and I will give you rest. Take my yoke upon you and learn from me, for I am gentle and humble in heart, and you will find rest for your souls. For my yoke is easy and my burden is light."
MATTHEW 11:28–30 NIV

Sometimes life seems like a race that you can never win. . .and you get tired. Overwhelmed. Bone-weary. Your busyness matters to Jesus. He wants you to come to Him and rest in Him daily, finding a new and less hurried rhythm of grace.

The Amplified Classic Bible expounds on what this means. The kind of rest Jesus offers is this: "relief and ease and refreshment and recreation and blessed quiet" (verse 29). We're not talking about heaven here. This is the peace that Jesus offers you right now! And the "yoke" he wants to give you is this: "useful, good—not harsh, hard, sharp, or pressing, but comfortable, gracious, and pleasant" (verse 30 AMPC).

Jesus, please help me to find true rest and peace in You, in every circumstance, in every way.

DOUBTS

Then He said to Thomas, "Reach here with your finger, and see My hands; and put out your hand and place it in My side. Do not be unbelieving, but [stop doubting and] believe."

John 20:27 AMP

Jesus wants to make Himself known to you. He understands why you are the way you are, and He has great compassion for you. He is listening and He loves you more than you could ever imagine.

Remember that Jesus was willing to let Thomas touch His scars because that is what Thomas needed. You are His child, and He knows exactly what you need. He knows your heart. He will never abandon you. Even those painful things that happen in life, God will miraculously turn into good things if you trust in Him (Romans 8:28).

A lot of distractions will be coming at you always, trying to get you to doubt God's love for you. Ask the Holy Spirit to remind you of His amazing love whenever you start to doubt.

God, help me never to doubt Your amazing love and compassion for me! Thank You for knowing exactly what I need.

THE MERCY OF GOD

"But go and learn what this means: 'I desire mercy, not sacrifice.' For I have not come to call the righteous, but sinners."
MATTHEW 9:13 NIV

The Pharisees were upset that Jesus was befriending "sinners" and people they would have had nothing to do with. The Pharisees considered themselves above others because they stringently kept all of the rules. They were righteous—self-righteous.

Jesus clarified that He didn't come to call people who are already righteous. Righteous people don't need anything but their own rules and other people to notice how well they do at keeping them. Jesus came for the lost and the broken. The needy and the hopeless. Those who are honest about their failings and come up short.

Thankfully, God is rich in mercy. He delights in showing it. Jesus wants us to study the mercy of God. Learn what it means. Accept it gratefully, and dish it out abundantly.

We both know I don't deserve Your mercy, Lord. But I am thankful. Help me show mercy to others as I point them to You.

LOVE FROM THE WOMB

Have mercy on me, my God, have mercy on me, for in you I take refuge. I will take refuge in the shadow of your wings until the disaster has passed.

PSALM 57:1 NIV

The Hebrew word for "mercy" is derived from the word for "womb." When you think about how a baby cannot survive outside of the mother's womb, it's similar to the merciful love that God offers to us. A loving pregnant mother makes sacrifices, changes her diet, and does everything she can to keep the baby safe. Her body provides all the baby needs to live and be healthy. If the baby leaves the protection of the womb too soon, it will die.

God's mercy means love, protection, nourishment, and sacrifice. Maybe this is another reason Jesus told us to study the mercy of God. It's so much more than we think! David ran to this protective and loving mercy of God. Will you? Pastor Robert Gelinas has said, "The closer you get to God, the more mercy—love from the womb—you get from Him."

Lord, I want to know more of Your mercy. I need Your protection and Your very life to sustain me.

THE GREAT I AM

God replied to Moses, "I AM WHO I AM. Say this to the people of Israel: I AM has sent me to you."
EXODUS 3:14 NLT

Our hope for life is never about what we can do. Our hope is in Christ alone. No matter how many things we accomplish for Jesus, our confidence, strength, and ability come from Him. He is the great I Am. He is who He says He is. He can do all the things He has ever done. . .and He can do them all again! What God says He will do, He does.

God's Word is on the line here. He is committed to loving you, saving you, redeeming you, and finishing everything He started when you said yes to Him. He will never give up on you.

If you struggle with feeling unloved, you can rest in the truth that God is committed to you and will never leave you alone. He loves you with an everlasting love that will not change with your feelings.

Lord God, I worship You alone. You are the great I Am. And I believe You are who You say You are!

LOVER OF GOD

Now may the Lord of peace Himself grant you His peace at all times and in every way [that peace and spiritual well-being that comes to those who walk with Him, regardless of life's circumstances]. The Lord be with you all.

2 THESSALONIANS 3:16 AMP

We often go to Jesus when we want something. But if we treated our friends on earth this way, they likely wouldn't be good friends for long. Consider this: How often do you go to Jesus just to be with Him? To worship Him?

Today's verse talks about God's peace. It is part of a spiritual well-being that comes from just walking with God. Being with Him. Loving Him. Not asking for anything this time. Just thankfully spending time with Him in worship.

Prayerfully consider ways that, instead of just being a good Christian, you can focus on being a lover of God.

Lord, I want to walk with You and be Your friend. I want to love You with my whole heart.

TELL YOUR STORY

Has the Lord *redeemed you? Then speak out!*
Tell others he has redeemed you from your enemies.
Psalm 107:2 NLT

The New International Version says, "Let the redeemed of the Lord tell their story." Louie Giglio rightly says that we all have the same story: "We were dead and now we're not." But the unique story that God has written in your life can be a catalyst for others in ways you never thought possible. It has been said that "your story could be the key to unlocking someone else's prison."

Our stories are important. God wants to use every piece of what you've gone through to bring others to His loving and saving grace.

When was the last time you shared what God has done in you? If you struggle with vulnerability, ask God for courage. He loves to dish it out in excess. As His Spirit works in you, teaching you what to say at just the right time (Luke 12:12), you'll be amazed at what He can do with your story in the lives of others.

Use my story, Lord. Please fill me with courage to be vulnerable.

CAST AND RELEASE

Cast your burden on the Lord [release it] and He will sustain and uphold you; He will never allow the righteous to be shaken (slip, fall, fail). . . . But I will [boldly and unwaveringly] trust in You.

Psalm 55:22–23 AMP

How many times have you recalled the verse "Cast all your anxiety on him because he cares for you" (1 Peter 5:7 NIV)? It's a great verse to remember, and if you grew up in church, you probably memorized it as a child.

Here's what a lot of us do: We remember the verse as the Holy Spirit brings it to our minds. Then we take our cares to God in prayer. We may leave them there for a minute. But more often than not, we take our worries and anxieties right back as soon as we say "Amen."

Psalm 55 in the Amplified Bible gives us a better idea: Cast your burdens and cares on God. . .and then release them! Don't reel them back in as soon as you're done praying! He promises to uphold you as you unwaveringly trust in Him.

Lord, it's hard for me to leave my worries with You. Please help me trust You more.

YOU BELONG

I want you to think about how all this makes you more significant, not less. A body isn't just a single part blown up into something huge. It's all the different-but-similar parts arranged and functioning together.
1 CORINTHIANS 12:14–15 MSG

Have you ever walked into a room and felt instantly like you didn't belong? That can happen in groups and in social settings, but it should never happen around other believers. Why? Because you fit together with fellow Christians. You are a part of God's body. And you belong because God says you do.

As believers in Jesus Christ, we all form one body. The body of Christ. We all need each other to move and grow. Each part is distinct and important. The next time you feel intimidated or unwelcome at a church function, ask Jesus to give you courage and show you your purpose there. If you are feeling unwelcome, maybe it's because God wants you to help welcome others!

Lord, thanks for giving me a place in Your body. Remind me that I belong because I'm a part of You.

CHOSEN

"You did not choose me, but I chose you and appointed you that you should go and bear fruit and that your fruit should abide, so that whatever you ask the Father in my name, he may give it to you."

JOHN 15:16 ESV

Did you know that God chose you? Yes, you. The Bible says that He chose you before the creation of the world! Check it out: "For he chose us in him before the creation of the world to be holy and blameless in his sight" (Ephesians 1:4 NIV).

Sit with that thought for a minute. Imagine God creating the whole world and already knowing you would be a part of it, His beloved child! It's mind-blowing!

Whenever you struggle with believing any truth from God's Word, dig in. Ask God to show you why you struggle and to heal that area in your heart. You are chosen. You are loved. God knew about you long before you were born. He has great plans for your life. Believe it.

I'm so amazed that You really chose me to be Your child, Lord. Thank You!

THE QUESTION

When Jesus noticed him lying there [helpless], knowing that he had been in that condition a long time, He said to him, "Do you want to get well?"
JOHN 5:6 AMP

Jesus saw a lame man lying by the healing pool. He was trapped by his body and had been for nearly forty years. His hopelessness was a part of him. It was the only way he knew to live. So why would Jesus ask him if he wanted to get well?

Is it possible that some people prefer to stay stuck? Maybe it's easier and safer, in their minds, to live life the way they always have. Change is hard. Even good change causes stress and involves a lot of unknowns. So Jesus was asking a deep question: Do you really want to get well?

What about you? Are you feeling stuck in some way and lack the "oomph" to say yes to the next right step? Imagine Jesus holding His hand out to you and asking you this same question. How will you respond?

Jesus, I don't want to be stuck in the same patterns of thinking that caused my trouble in the first place. Please help me to get well.

COMPLETE

For in Him all the fullness of Deity (the Godhead) dwells in bodily form [completely expressing the divine essence of God]. And in Him you have been made complete [achieving spiritual stature through Christ], and He is the head over all rule and authority [of every angelic and earthly power].

COLOSSIANS 2:9–10 AMP

In Christ alone, you are complete. No human being can complete you. God never meant for any of us to put that responsibility on another human being. It's too much for human shoulders. Romantic movies may try to tell us otherwise, but people will often fail us and let us down. And that's okay. We can have grace for others and their human failings. But when our expectations of others are too high, our idols fall and then we're lost and disappointed.

Only Jesus has shoulders big enough to carry us. When you are whole in Christ, you can be in relationship with others in healthy and loving ways, with mutual responsibility for the success of the relationship.

Lord, I repent of placing too many expectations on others instead of allowing You to complete me.

ALL THINGS ARE POSSIBLE

Jesus looked at them and said, "With man this is impossible, but with God all things are possible."
MATTHEW 19:26 ESV

The Message has a noteworthy way of putting it: "No chance at all if you think you can pull it off yourself. Every chance in the world if you trust God to do it." When you're in a seemingly impossible situation, it's easy to begin measuring your strength against the circumstances. But all through the Bible, God gives us example after example of how He shows up for His people in astounding ways when they trust Him. Your strength will never be enough. God's strength always is.

When you pray, everything is possible! Because "impossible" is God's specialty! Nothing is ever too big for Him, and nothing too small!

Jesus, I want to trust You more. Help me come to You, knowing that You are everything I need and that nothing is impossible with You.

GOD IS CLOSE

The eyes of the LORD watch over those who do right; his ears are open to their cries for help. . . . The LORD is close to the brokenhearted; he rescues those whose spirits are crushed.

PSALM 34:15, 18 NLT

When you read God's Word, you come to realize that God desires to be with people! It's true.

Jesus is closer than you think. When your heart is broken, He is with you. When your spirit feels crushed, God is close. His Word says that He hears your prayers and His eyes are on you. He sees you. You are important to God and He loves you more than you could ever imagine.

God loves to send little reminders and blessings your way. Sometimes He will send someone to give you an extra-special dose of love at just the right time. Sometimes He will supernaturally warm your heart with love as you talk to Him. Be on the lookout for His love.

Jesus, thank You for seeing me and sending blessings and reminders that You are close.

THE GOD OF ANGEL ARMIES

"'Yes, get to work! For I am with you.' The God-of-the-Angel-Armies is speaking! 'Put into action the word I covenanted with you when you left Egypt. I'm living and breathing among you right now. Don't be timid. Don't hold back.'"

Haggai 2:5 msg

One of the names of God is Jehovah Sabaoth, translated as "Lord of Hosts" or "God of Angel Armies." The God of Angel Armies is your God too. He is with you and for you. He's living and breathing in you!

The Amplified Bible says, "My Spirit stands [firm and immovable] and continues with you; do not fear!" The firm and immovable God of all creation is standing right there with you. . .always. He will never ask you to go somewhere or do something where He is not. He will never abandon you.

Lord, You are the great God of Angel Armies. And yet You are alive and at work inside of me. That's so amazing! Thank You for never leaving my side and bringing me courage from Your strength.

MY STRENGTH AND PORTION

My flesh and my heart may fail, but God is the rock and strength of my heart and my portion forever.
Psalm 73:26 AMP

Sometimes our bodies and minds just give out. We mess up. We get it wrong. We fall. We see ourselves as failures. We will never be able to muster enough strength to carry all the burdens of this life ourselves. But instead of walking away in defeat and shame, you can lift your head. . .because of Jesus.

God sees you through the perfect lens of Jesus. He sees you as whole and beautiful and perfect through the righteousness of Christ alone. Jesus' redemption of you cost Him everything, so please don't take it for granted. He wants you to walk in His freedom and strength. He paid dearly for it.

God can and will use every failure to point to His strength, if you let Him. So lift your head and allow Him to lead you forward.

Jesus, the price You paid for my freedom is unfathomable. I will trust You to make something beautiful out of my mistakes. I release them into Your hands so that You can do the work that only You can do.

WELCOMED AND LOVED

There is no fear in love, but perfect love casts out fear. For fear has to do with punishment, and whoever fears has not been perfected in love. We love because he first loved us.

1 JOHN 4:18–19 ESV

The major blessing of our lives is that we have access to God. We can always approach Him without fear because He sees us through the love and sacrifice of Jesus. Jesus made a way to reconcile us with the Father, once and for all. So God is not angry with you. He is a good Father, longing to hold you close and love you well all the days of your life.

You don't have to work harder or be a better Christian to earn God's love. When you begin to believe who you are in Christ, this thinking changes everything. You start living differently. You realize how deeply you are loved, and that love sets you free. As Jesus pours His love and His Spirit into your life, they spill over into the lives of those around you.

You are my good, good Father. I'm so thankful I am welcomed and loved in Your presence.

THE WORK OF BELIEVING: PART 1

Jesus answered them, "This is the work of God, that you believe in him whom he has sent."
JOHN 6:29 ESV

In John 6, crowds of people were looking for Jesus. He had recently fed them all, and they were hungry again. Jesus tells them not to work for food that spoils, but to work for spiritual food. They're not quite sure what Jesus is saying, so they ask, "What must we do to do the works God requires?" (John 6:28 NIV). Isn't this a common question among Christians? Especially women? What do we need to do next?

Does Jesus' answer surprise you? The work is simply to believe.

That may sound easy enough. So why does Jesus call it work? What is the work of believing? It's definitely not striving. It's not following a list of rules. It's not signing up for anything and everything at church.

It's simple enough for a child to understand, but also the most challenging choice of all: choosing faith every moment, every day. Let's take a deeper look at this subject tomorrow.

Jesus, I want to know Your plan for me and follow it wholeheartedly.

THE WORK OF BELIEVING: PART 2

So keep at your work, this faith and love rooted in Christ, exactly as I set it out for you. It's as sound as the day you first heard it from me. Guard this precious thing placed in your custody by the Holy Spirit who works in us.

2 TIMOTHY 1:14 MSG

The work of believing will be a journey of discovery for all followers of Jesus. A one-size-fits-all list for Christians will never do. Each person must cultivate their faith and guard it well, rooting themselves in the love of Christ.

Growing an everyday, moment-by-moment faith takes work. Having faith isn't always easy—especially during difficult times. Aligning your heart and mind with God's truth when the whole world is telling you otherwise takes courage and strength. Thankfully, we've learned where the power to do that comes from.

As we continue taking our thoughts captive and allowing Jesus to live out His very life in and through us, we trust and rest in Him. And His Spirit provides the power and ability to carry out all of His purposes for our lives.

Thank You for giving my life purpose, Jesus.
I will join You in Your work.

HEAVENLY COUNSEL

I will instruct you and teach you in the way you should go; I will counsel you with my loving eye on you.

PSALM 32:8 NIV

What a blessing that we have direct access to the God who knows everything and can do everything! He always sees the big picture. He always wants the best for you. And He always wins His battles.

When you are frustrated and feel stuck in your circumstances, you can take a step back and look up. Remember that God Himself wants to counsel you, teach you, and guide you. He is there and He wants to help. The more you go to Him with everything, the more you will begin to see Him act on your behalf.

Are you doing the work of believing? What is stopping you?

Go to Jesus in prayer and bring these questions before Him. Ask for help with any problems you are currently facing. Write down the date and be on the lookout for ways God wants to answer and bless you for coming to Him.

Lord God, I'm so thankful that You want to hear from me! I'm asking for help. Please counsel me.

BLESSING OTHERS

You were cleansed from your sins when you obeyed the truth, so now you must show sincere love to each other as brothers and sisters. Love each other deeply with all your heart.

1 PETER 1:22 NLT

People move in and out of your life for a purpose. Every human being you interact with on a daily basis is someone to whom you can show God's love. If you're in the drive-through line to get your coffee, greet the person with a smile and pray a blessing over them in your heart as they take care of you. Do the same as you wait in line at the grocery store.

Aim to bless each person you come into contact with in this way. Bless instead of complain. Pray and show love instead of getting impatient when your schedule or agenda is interrupted.

Lord, I'm sorry I get impatient with others when things aren't going my way. Help me look around and bless all the people You put in my path. They are there for a reason. Help me see them the way You do.

BORN TO CHANGE THE WORLD

And he said to them, "Go into all the world and proclaim the gospel to the whole creation."
MARK 16:15 ESV

Did you know that God created you to be transformed? He didn't just make people to be born, grow into adults, work, make money, die. . .and that's the end of the story. Nope! And aren't you so glad? You were created to be a fearless world-changer!

And changing the world begins at home. As you live a life of being loved by God, His love overflows to others in your home and your areas of influence, who in turn are affected by that supernatural love. Little by little, this powerful love changes the lives of those who are blessed by it.

You were born to bless and change the world. One person at a time.

I'm Yours, Lord. Help me love and bless others well so that I can make a difference in the lives of the people around me.

HIDE OR SEEK

"Starting from scratch, he made the entire human race and made the earth hospitable, with plenty of time and space for living so we could seek after God, and not just grope around in the dark but actually find him. He doesn't play hide-and-seek with us. He's not remote; he's near. We live and move in him, can't get away from him!"

ACTS 17:25–26 MSG

Humans like to hide when they feel like they're not measuring up or are failing completely. We also hide when we are knowingly choosing sin. Maybe you're involved in something you see as no big deal, but actually it is putting up a wall between you and God.

God is close. He sees you. He wants you to come to Him with your struggles so that He can help you overcome.

How have you walked away from God recently? Do you need to search your heart? Can you think of anything you need to repent of ? Ask Jesus to bring any darkness to light as you go to Him in prayer.

Lord, I repent of hiding from You. I want Your will and Your ways in my life.

GOD IS SOVEREIGN

The Lord has established His throne in the heavens,
and His sovereignty rules over all [the universe].
Psalm 103:19 AMP

If you believe in the sovereignty of God, you know there was never a plan B. Everlasting life in Him was always the plan before the creation of the world. He knew humans would mess up. He wasn't surprised when Adam and Eve sinned. He knew sin would be devastating if He gave us all a choice. But love was worth it.

Many of us have a lot of regrets and failures in life we wish we could go back and undo, but God uses them all. He makes all things work together for good. And as Isaiah 61:3 (NIV) tells us, He came "to bestow on them a crown of beauty instead of ashes, the oil of joy instead of mourning, and a garment of praise instead of a spirit of despair."

Instead of looking back on your cringe-worthy memories in shame, ask Jesus to keep turning those failures into garments of praise.

Sovereign Lord, please take my ashes and turn them into something beautiful, to be used for Your glory.

I TRUST IN YOU

But I trust in you, Lord; I say, "You are my God." My times are in your hands.
Psalm 31:14–15 NIV

C. H. Spurgeon said, "The worst calamity is the wisest and the kindest thing that could befall to me—if God ordains it." Can you receive the worst disaster as a gift from God? It seems like a lot to ask.

Fanny Crosby, the great hymnwriter, came to see her blindness as a gift from God. She went on to write: "Blessed assurance, Jesus is mine. . . . Perfect submission, all is at rest; I in my Savior, am happy and blessed. Watching and waiting, looking above, filled with His goodness, lost in His love. This is my story, this is my song, praising my Savior all the day long." She said she was thankful for her blindness because the first face she would see was her Lord's when she got to heaven.

When you place your pain in God's loving hands, you can be at rest in your Savior too.

Jesus, I bring You my pain. Help me to trust Your goodness through it all.

A SHIELD OF FAVOR

But let all who take refuge and put their trust in You rejoice, let them ever sing for joy; because You cover and shelter them, let those who love Your name be joyful and exult in You. For You, O Lord, bless the righteous man [the one who is in right standing with You]; You surround him with favor as with a shield.

Psalm 5:11–12 AMP

The Bible talks about reaping what you sow. If you've sown the fruits of the Spirit in your heart, those fruits of love, joy, peace, patience, kindness, goodness, gentleness, faithfulness, and self-control start growing (Galatians 5:22–23). And you reap God's protection and blessing.

Yes, life can be hard. Pulling weeds and tending the garden of your life can be difficult work. But you are not doing it alone. Jesus Himself gives you His mighty resurrection power to keep going. He shields you with His favor. And you will reap His blessings even in the midst of struggles.

I want Your blessing and shield over my life, Lord. But more than that, please give me the desire to want You alone. Your presence is the blessing. Your presence is the shield.

MY IMPENETRABLE SHIELD

The LORD is my strength and my [impenetrable] shield;
my heart trusts [with unwavering confidence] in Him,
and I am helped; therefore my heart greatly rejoices,
and with my song I shall thank Him and praise Him.

PSALM 28:7 AMP

When you allow Jesus to be your source of strength, He also becomes a shield that nothing can get past without His consent. He is your hiding place, and you can run to Him anytime, for anything. With His mighty power, He shields you from every attack that comes against you.

Isaiah 54:17 (NIV) says, "'No weapon forged against you will prevail, and you will refute every tongue that accuses you. This is the heritage of the servants of the LORD, and this is their vindication from me,' declares the LORD."

You are a child of God with a rich heritage. Your citizenship is in heaven and you've been adopted by God Himself. You are safe.

Jesus, I'm so thankful that my heritage comes from You. You cancel attacks and assignments from the enemy that have been sent my way. I trust that You will shield and protect me.

GOD IN A BOX

Great indeed, we confess, is the mystery of godliness: He was manifested in the flesh, vindicated by the Spirit, seen by angels, proclaimed among the nations, believed on in the world, taken up in glory.

1 TIMOTHY 3:16 ESV

Humans like to solve puzzles and make sense of complicated subjects. We take pride in it. Theologians and biblical scholars sometimes might pride themselves on their great knowledge of God. The wisest followers of Jesus, though, know that you can't put God in a box or put limits on what He can do.

Jesus wants our faith to resemble that of childlike wonder. Jesus said in Matthew 18:3 (NIV), "Truly I tell you, unless you change and become like little children, you will never enter the kingdom of heaven."

Repent of putting limits on God. Ask Him to break down any walls you've constructed that prevent Him from fully accessing your heart.

Spirit of God, rise up in me. Help me trust that You are the God of miracles and that You are personally interested in everything about me.

STRENGTH AND POWER

Do you not know? Have you not heard? The LORD is the everlasting God, the Creator of the ends of the earth. He will not grow tired or weary, and his understanding no one can fathom. He gives strength to the weary and increases the power of the weak.

ISAIAH 40:28–29 NIV

The Message says that God "energizes those who get tired, gives fresh strength to dropouts" (verse 29). Have you ever felt like a dropout of the faith? Don't beat yourself up for being human. Jesus wants you to come to Him exactly as you are and work things out with Him. God wants your heart, not your perfect behavior.

If you messed up today, or you've been messing up every day. . .bring it all to Jesus. There's no need to hide it, because He already knows. Ask Him to search your heart. Give Him permission to help you sort it all out. All of the strength and power you'll ever need is found in Him.

Lord, please search my heart today. I need Your help to sort things out. Please renew my strength.

STRENGTH FROM THE GOD WHO SPEAKS

It is God who arms me with strength
and keeps my way secure.
PSALM 18:32 NIV

God arms us with strength. The Passion Translation of this verse says that God wraps us in power. The Bible uses a lot of imagery to connect us with God more fully. Read through all of Psalm 18. Now close your eyes and picture what God is saying. Can you see Jesus arming you with strength as He wraps you in His power? What does God want you to know about this passage of scripture specifically as it pertains to you? Ask Him.

We worship a God who loves to speak and give clarity to His children. He is not silent. You can hear Him speaking in thousands of ways all day long, if you're listening. Be still. . .do you hear Him speaking to your heart today?

Lord, I'm so thankful for all of the ways You speak to me, wrapping me in strength as You do.

FOR SUCH A TIME AS THIS

"If you persist in staying silent at a time like this, help and deliverance will arrive for the Jews from someplace else; but you and your family will be wiped out. Who knows? Maybe you were made queen for just such a time as this."

ESTHER 4:13–14 MSG

Do you believe that you were created with a purpose? You're not just here by chance. You were formed by a heavenly Creator who made you exactly the woman you are. And He created you for this specific time and place.

God has used His people throughout history for His special plan and purpose. Esther was an orphan, raised by her Jewish uncle, and God gave her supernatural courage to save His people from annihilation. As He did for Esther, God has a special purpose for you too. You are where you are right now for a reason.

Lord, I trust that You have a great purpose for my life. Please give me the courage I need to carry it out.

HAVE YOU MISSED THE POINT?

Because of his great love for us, God, who is rich in mercy, made us alive with Christ even when we were dead in transgressions—it is by grace you have been saved.

Ephesians 2:4–5 NIV

Growing up in an evangelical church is an awesome blessing. But sometimes you hear so much about going and telling and making disciples that you completely miss the point that the gospel is for you too.

Going and telling and sharing the gospel with the world is God's great commission to His followers. But you can't do that effectively if your own heart hasn't been affected.

Spend some time reading Psalm 139 today. Allow this message from God to wash over your heart:

He loves *you*. He sees *you*. He wants a relationship with *you*.

You are His beloved. *You* matter to God. *You* are worth dying for.

Many Christians tend to do and do until the exhaustion point. But the way of Jesus is to get filled up by His love first. As you are filled more and more with His love, you will have reserves to offer others.

Jesus, I don't want to miss the point.
Let Your love change me first.

STILL BEFORE GOD

Be still before the LORD and wait patiently for him.

PSALM 37:7 NIV

Many of us like to skip right over this instruction to "be still."

It's hard. We're busy. We're doing good things. There is a lot of work to get done. I have to. . . I'm expected to. . . No one else can. . . And on and on.

The instruction to be still before God is not meant to be guilt inducing. It's actually for *you*. For your good. To bring you blessing and to fill your heart with love and peace.

Quieting your mind before God, just sitting in His presence and asking Him to be real to you, is where real, everyday faith begins. Our culture is one of distraction and selfishness. Unless you carve out some time to be still, the enemy will do everything he can to keep it from happening.

This is not a simple checkbox on your to-do list. It's faith in action. And it's spiritual warfare. As you prep yourself for the daily spiritual battles of this world, remember the most important first step: Be still. Be filled by His love.

Lord Jesus, please stir in my heart a strong desire to be still before You and hear Your voice before I face today's battles.

A DAY TO PRAISE

My tongue will proclaim your righteousness,
your praises all day long.
Psalm 35:28 niv

There is so much goodness to be found if we're looking for it. Take a day to praise God and keep a thankful heart. Think of our amazing heavenly Father and all the wonders He has provided. Let the worship music flow as you go about your day, and meditate on these scriptures:

- "I will be glad and rejoice in you; I will sing the praises of your name, O Most High" (Psalm 9:2 niv).
- "I will sing the Lord's praise, for he has been good to me" (Psalm 13:6 niv).
- "I will praise the Lord, who counsels me; even at night my heart instructs me" (Psalm 16:7 niv).
- "Be exalted in your strength, Lord; we will sing and praise your might" (Psalm 21:13 niv).
- "Praise be to the Lord, for he has heard my cry for mercy" (Psalm 28:6 niv).
- "In God we make our boast all day long, and we will praise your name forever" (Psalm 44:8 niv).

I praise Your great name, Lord God. I'm so thankful for who You are and what You've done.

GOD'S PROMISES BRING HOPE

For great is your love, reaching to the heavens;
your faithfulness reaches to the skies. Be exalted, O God,
above the heavens; let your glory be over all the earth.
PSALM 57:10–11 NIV

David was hiding out in fear for his life as Saul and his men pursued him. David knew that only God could save him from being killed by his enemies. So he prayed. He cried out to God and worshipped Him. This psalm is part of David's desperate prayer. After he poured out his heart to God and laid out all of his fears, he began to praise God and remember all of His promises.

Life can get pretty dark sometimes. But there is great power in our prayers as we stand on the promises of God. God came through for David that day in the cave (1 Samuel 24).

When you feel like you want to run and hide, pour out your heart to God. Ask for His help. Declare His promises. Then watch Him work.

I declare Your goodness and faithfulness,
Lord God. Nothing is impossible for You.

SUPERNATURAL HOPE

Not only so, but we also glory in our sufferings,
because we know that suffering produces perseverance;
perseverance, character; and character, hope.

ROMANS 5:3–4 NIV

Have you ever noticed in God's Word that we see more instances of God being with His people *through* painful times than keeping His people *from* difficult or dangerous circumstances?

When people run out of hope, they give up. It happens in sports. It happens in life. But when people can hold on to even a glimmer of hope, they have strength to keep going.

Jesus is always offering us supernatural hope to help us keep on keeping on. He comforts us in our pain. His supernatural presence sustains us. He wants to pour His hope into your heart so that you can offer it to others who are close to giving up.

Romans 5:5 in the Amplified Bible says, "Such hope [in God's promises] never disappoints us, because God's love has been abundantly poured out within our hearts through the Holy Spirit who was given to us."

My only hope is in You, Lord. Pour Your love into my heart continually so that I can offer Your hope to those who need it.

Clearing the Air

So now there is no condemnation for those who belong to Christ Jesus. And because you belong to him, the power of the life-giving Spirit has freed you from the power of sin that leads to death.

Romans 8:1–2 NLT

There is no safer, no better, no freer, no more powerful place to be than near to Jesus. Romans 8:1–2 in The Message says we "no longer have to live under a continuous, low-lying black cloud. A new power is in operation. The Spirit of life in Christ, like a strong wind, has magnificently cleared the air, freeing you from a fated lifetime of brutal tyranny at the hands of sin and death."

No more black clouds. No more condemnation. No more guilt and shame. Instead, Jesus has cleared the air. You are free.

Do you believe it? Are you walking out your faith in that truth? Bring these thoughts to Jesus. If you struggle with walking in true freedom, ask Jesus to reveal His truth to you.

Jesus, I want to walk in freedom as I follow You. Please show me the way.

PRAYER IN BATTLE

"For the LORD your God is going with you! He will fight for you against your enemies, and he will give you victory!"
DEUTERONOMY 20:4 NLT

Spiritual warfare is real. The Bible tells us to be alert because our enemy prowls around looking to devour us (1 Peter 5:8). The Bible also tells us that our battle exists in the unseen world (Ephesians 6:12).

Do you ever struggle with fears and worries? Fear can be a real battle for a woman, and it is one of our enemy's main schemes against us. But we don't fight this battle in our own strength. Prayer changes everything.

We pray because we can't handle everything on our own. And through prayer, we access the power of God to help us stand firm against the attacks of the enemy.

Say a prayer of thanks today, for God has given us everything we need to overcome. Take a look at Ephesians 6:10–18. Ask the Holy Spirit to teach you what you need to know to help conquer your fears.

Jesus, I'm so thankful for Your provision and blessing. In Your strength, I overcome.

HELP IN TIMES OF TROUBLE

God is our refuge and strength,
an ever-present help in trouble.
PSALM 46:1 NIV

Take a look at the story of Elijah in 1 Kings 19. He was so done with his difficult and exhausting life that he asked God to let him die. Imagine the utter defeat and despair he was feeling. But God saw Elijah. He knew exactly what he needed. So He sent an angel to feed and minister to him. Some of us can relate to Elijah a little. . .or maybe even a lot.

Life gets tough and even the most courageous of us get knocked down, with little left to give it another go. But that's the very place where we find that our courage was never our own anyway.

God is our ever-present help and the source of our courage. We can hide away in Him. And He gives us the supernatural help we need to get back up again.

He did it for Elijah. He has done it for untold numbers of His children throughout the centuries. And He can do the same for you.

God, thank You for seeing my need and sending help.

REMEMBER GOD'S FAITHFULNESS

"God, who delivered me from the teeth of the lion and the claws of the bear, will deliver me from this Philistine."
1 Samuel 17:37 msg

Verses 32–33 tell more of the story: "'Master,' said David, 'don't give up hope. I'm ready to go and fight this Philistine.' Saul answered David, 'You can't go and fight this Philistine. You're too young and inexperienced—and he's been at this fighting business since before you were born.'"

As you journey in faith, it becomes so important to remember God's faithfulness to you specifically. David wasn't afraid of Goliath because he remembered how God had been faithful to him so many times in the past.

Take some time to begin recording the big things you've seen God do in your life. Write down dates if you know them, or your best guess. Then commit to journaling how God shows up in your life. And when life seems hard and you need more courage and faith. . .you have a black-and-white reminder of how God has been real to you in the past.

Lord, thank You for Your great faithfulness to me.

THE POWER OF GOD

"LORD, the God of our ancestors, are you not the God who is in heaven? You rule over all the kingdoms of the nations. Power and might are in your hand, and no one can withstand you."

2 CHRONICLES 20:6 NIV

In 1 Kings 18 we see a dramatic display of God's power. Elijah didn't have any doubt in the almighty power of God. God spoke to Elijah and Elijah obeyed. He knew God's voice. Elijah told the truth with courage and boldness that came because he trusted God. God showed up, just like Elijah knew He would.

In verse 37 (NLT) Elijah calls to God: "O LORD, answer me! Answer me so these people will know that you, O LORD, are God and that you have brought them back to yourself."

Immediately, fire flashed from heaven and burned up the sacrifice, even licking up the water in the trench. All of the people fell down and marveled at God's raw power.

Where do you need God to show up in a big way right now? Talk to Him about it.

Lord, please give me boldness like Elijah's and an unwavering faith in You.

STROLLING AT LEISURE

Your vows are binding upon me, O God; I will give thank offerings to You. For You have rescued my soul from death, yes, and my feet from stumbling, so that I may walk before God in the light of life.

Psalm 56:12–13 AMP

Did you ever stop to think what hurrying ever really accomplishes in life? Think about your most hectic days and what the outcome was. Did you grow more in your faith? Did you spend quality one-on-one time with the heavenly Father? Did you take time to really listen to a family member's thoughts and feelings?

Jesus took His time with people. He was intentional about everything He did and said. Overloading your schedule and rushing to get everything done only causes anxiety.

Take a deep breath and look at your schedule. What can you prayerfully eliminate to create more breathing room in your life?

Psalm 56:12–13 (MSG) says, "God, you did everything you promised, and I'm thanking you with all my heart. You pulled me from the brink of death, my feet from the cliff-edge of doom. Now I stroll at leisure with God in the sunlit fields of life."

Lord, I want to spend more time strolling with You. Help me slow down and eliminate unnecessary things from my schedule.

START AND END WITH BLESSING

Jesus went throughout all the cities and villages [in Galilee], teaching in their synagogues and proclaiming the good news (gospel) of the kingdom, and healing every kind of disease and every kind of sickness [His words and His works reflecting His Messiahship].

MATTHEW 9:35 AMP

In Matthew 5:3 (AMP) Jesus says, "Blessed [spiritually prosperous, happy, to be admired] are the poor in spirit [those devoid of spiritual arrogance, those who regard themselves as insignificant], for theirs is the kingdom of heaven [both now and forever]."

Jesus wants to bless your life. Even in trials and pain, He is there, offering His hope and His presence. Being blessed doesn't mean enjoying a life completely devoid of sorrow, but rather knowing that the almighty Creator has your hand firmly in His, leading you along life's path with supernatural joy and peace. And this abundant life, in turn, gives courage to others whose lives have been marked by suffering.

Thank You for the blessing of Your presence, God. Allow my life and my story to bring the hope of Your peace to others.

THE JOY OF WORK

The LORD God took the man and put him in the Garden of Eden to work it and take care of it.

GENESIS 2:15 NIV

Before the fall of mankind, there was work to be done in the perfect Garden of Eden. Adam and Eve worked and ruled together. Work is a gift and a blessing, allowing us to use the strength and fortitude God has given us to do a job well. A sense of accomplishment blesses us and helps us enjoy times of rest and play even more.

See your work as a blessing today. Know that God has called you to complete tasks for His Kingdom, and He's given you the talent and skills and strength to do them. There's nothing like a day of hard work followed by a good night's rest!

Lord, thank You for the gift of work. I'm thankful You've given me something for my hands and mind to do, and even then, I can worship as I work.

GOD'S LIFE-MAP BRINGS JOY

The revelation of God is whole and pulls our lives together.
The signposts of God are clear and point out the right road.
The life-maps of God are right, showing the way to joy.
Psalm 19:7–8 msg

Our God is a good Dad! He's a perfect, wise, and loving parent to us no matter our age. He doesn't give us rules and guidelines to spoil our fun or make us miserable. The exact opposite is true! Just like a wise parent gives their children rules and good boundaries to keep them healthy and safe, so does our loving heavenly Father. But the choice to follow is ours alone.

The Bible tells us that following God's life-map for us will lead us to joy. God's Word can bring us a daily sense of gratitude and freedom if we allow it to.

Are you carrying any resentment toward God right now? Are you conflicted about God's boundaries and guidelines for you? Bring these thoughts to Jesus. Ask Him to give you His perspective and to plant seeds of joy in your heart as you follow His life-map for you.

Thank You for Your plan for me, Lord God.
Help me follow with a grateful heart.

HAPPY IN THE LORD

Trust in the Lord, and do good. So you will live in the land and will be fed. Be happy in the Lord. And He will give you the desires of your heart.

PSALM 37:3–4 NLV

When you begin to trust God more fully, you'll start to see little blessings everywhere. As you follow Jesus, He begins transforming you day by day through the power of the Holy Spirit alive inside of you. You'll notice that your heart is changing to want what Jesus wants for you, instead of your own selfish desires.

Being happy in the Lord is a choice. You can choose to begin each morning with thankfulness, no matter the circumstances. You can choose to see your life from an eternal perspective.

Commit your whole heart to the Lord. All of your plans and ideas too. Ask for opportunities to be a blessing to everyone around you. Talk to Jesus about each decision and problem you face. Then thank Him for the big and little blessings that come your way.

Lord Jesus, I commit my life to You. Help me choose to be happy in You each day.

FLOURISHING TREES

Oh, the joys of those who do not follow the advice of the wicked, or stand around with sinners, or join in with mockers. But they delight in the law of the LORD, meditating on it day and night. They are like trees planted along the riverbank, bearing fruit each season. Their leaves never wither, and they prosper in all they do.

PSALM 1:1–3 NLT

When we allow the Word of God to be a daily blessing in our lives, it helps us flourish like trees planted along the riverbank. The Amplified Bible puts verse 3 this way: "And in whatever he does, he prospers [and comes to maturity]."

Through the Holy Spirit, we have the very source of life itself alive and at work in us! So you can stop striving to make things work out on your own and rest in the fact that Jesus Himself will help you grow, prosper, and mature as you follow Him.

Lord, Your Word tells me in John 7:38 that rivers of living water will flow from within me as I follow You. Let Your Word and Your life renew me each day.

YOUR GIFTS ARE A BLESSING

"In the same way, let your light shine before others, that they may see your good deeds and glorify your Father in heaven."
MATTHEW 5:16 NIV

It's important to grow in the gifts that God has given you. Take a moment to jot down some of your God-given gifts and talents. The things that come easy to you and bring you joy. Many times we often neglect our talents because we don't have time for them. But God gave them to you for a reason.

First Timothy 4:14–15 (NLV) says, "Be sure to use the gift God gave you. The leaders saw this in you when they laid their hands on you and said what you should do. Think about all this. Work at it so everyone may see you are growing as a Christian."

Your talents were given to bring glory to God and enjoyment to you both. As you humbly offer your gifts and talents to God and others, your rewards are threefold: You bless the heart of God, you will be blessed yourself, and you'll be a blessing to others.

Thank You for my gifts, Lord. Help me use them for Your glory.

AN INNER CALM

Let the peace of Christ [the inner calm of one who walks daily with Him] be the controlling factor in your hearts [deciding and settling questions that arise]. To this peace indeed you were called as members in one body [of believers]. And be thankful [to God always].

COLOSSIANS 3:15 AMP

It's easy in today's world to have an underlying sense of foreboding. . .just waiting for the other shoe to drop at any moment. But that's not faith talking; that's fear. And living in fear is not the abundant life Jesus wants for you.

When you let the peace of Christ be the controlling factor in your heart, He gives you an inner calm as you walk daily with Him. As problems come, and they will, you trust in His power over every circumstance. You see life as an adventure of overcoming with Jesus. You anticipate challenges instead of fearing them, knowing that God will bring good out of everything that is submitted to Him.

Lord, I struggle with maintaining an inner calm. Please change my heart and help me trust You more.

STAY IN LOVE

Keep yourselves in the love of God, waiting for the mercy of our Lord Jesus Christ that leads to eternal life.
JUDE 21 ESV

This scripture from Jude 21 reminds us to keep ourselves in the love of God. Doing so requires a choice and an action on our part. Not mustering our own strength, but taking our thoughts captive, making them obedient to Christ, and aligning our hearts and minds with His truth. To simplify: When you have a negative thought, you take it to Jesus immediately and allow Him to remind you of His love for you and His truth.

In John 15:9–11 (NLV) Jesus says, "I have loved you just as My Father has loved Me. Stay in My love. If you obey My teaching, you will live in My love. In this way, I have obeyed My Father's teaching and live in His love. I have told you these things so My joy may be in you and your joy may be full."

Lord, change my heart and my thought-life to match Your loving truth.

EVERYDAY MIRACLES

"By faith in the name of Jesus, this man whom you see and know was made strong. It is Jesus' name and the faith that comes through him that has completely healed him, as you can all see."

ACTS 3:16 NIV

Do you believe in miracles? Have you ever personally experienced one, or do you know of someone who has?

Miracles are not a thing of the past—Bible times only. No, the things God has done before, He can still do. He is the same yesterday, today, and forever (Hebrews 13:8).

Is your heart open to God's miracles today? If you struggle with faith, talk to Jesus about this. He understands your fears and wants to help. Ask Him to remove any blinders you have and to fill your heart with thanksgiving.

Lord, I believe in You. Help me to trust Your power and Your goodness. Open my heart to thanksgiving and miracles.

BE HONEST

"Whoever can be trusted with very little can also be trusted with much, and whoever is dishonest with very little will also be dishonest with much."
LUKE 16:10 NIV

We know that telling the truth is very important to God. Ephesians 4:15 (AMP) says, "Speaking the truth in love [in all things—both our speech and our lives expressing His truth], let us grow up in all things into Him [following His example] who is the Head—Christ."

Being honest with others is critical. But being honest with ourselves and with God is essential too. Choosing to hide our hurts and wounds, instead of being honest with ourselves about how deeply we've been hurt or how much we are struggling, is a form of lying.

We don't want to hurt, so we pretend we aren't. But denial just makes it worse. Be honest with yourself and with God. Only then can He begin the work of healing in you that sets you free to grow and live an abundant life.

Lord, I'm sorry I've hidden my feelings. I need Your help to start being honest about them. I give You permission to help me deal with them and begin the healing process.

A HARVEST OF BLESSING

So let's not get tired of doing what is good. At just the right time we will reap a harvest of blessing if we don't give up. Therefore, whenever we have the opportunity, we should do good to everyone—especially to those in the family of faith.

GALATIANS 6:9–10 NLT

Always doing the right thing and "taking the high road" can be exhausting. Especially if you're trying to do those good things in your own strength. It takes supernatural strength to continue doing the right thing, being a woman of integrity, especially when no one is thanking you or paying any attention.

Remember as you do these things that Jesus is really the one you are serving, not people. As Colossians 3:23–24 (NIV) reminds us, "Whatever you do, work at it with all your heart, as working for the Lord, not for human masters, since you know that you will receive an inheritance from the Lord as a reward. It is the Lord Christ you are serving."

Lord, please help me not to give up. I need Your strength to keep doing the right thing. Remind me that You see me and my blessing comes from You.

LIKED BY GOD

"Worthy are You, our Lord and God, to receive the glory and the honor and the power; for You created all things, and because of Your will they exist, and were created and brought into being."
REVELATION 4:11 AMP

God created you to love you and delight in you. Just as loving parents long for children to love and enjoy, God feels this way about you too. Zephaniah 3:17 (NIV) tells us, "The LORD your God is with you, the Mighty Warrior who saves. He will take great delight in you; in his love he will no longer rebuke you, but will rejoice over you with singing."

God doesn't just love you. . .He likes you too. Is there anything more delightful?

What a blessing to know that you are loved and liked and enjoyed by God Himself. Allow these thoughts to stir up praise and thankfulness in your heart.

Lord God, I praise You for caring so much for me!

UNDER HIS WINGS

He will cover you and completely protect you with His pinions, and under His wings you will find refuge; His faithfulness is a shield and a wall.

PSALM 91:4 AMP

As you learn to go to Jesus with every thought and feeling, every heartache and concern, you will find that He wants to comfort and care for you. In Isaiah 66:13 (NIV), God says, "As a mother comforts her child, so will I comfort you."

Where do you need Jesus to cover you with His feathers and hide you under His wings? Journal about this today. Write down everything that comes to mind that is causing you frustration, fear, or anxiety.

God is faithful. As you let Him, He will shield you from harm and help you develop good and healthy boundaries that will serve you well in life.

Lord, what a beautiful picture that You allow me to hide under Your wings. I ask for Your protection and Your defense. I trust Your faithfulness to shield me from anything the enemy is throwing at me right now. Please help me make wise decisions with Your help.

MYSTERY AND POWER

Now to Him who is able to [carry out His purpose and] do superabundantly more than all that we dare ask or think [infinitely beyond our greatest prayers, hopes, or dreams], according to His power that is at work within us, to Him be the glory in the church and in Christ Jesus throughout all generations forever and ever. Amen.

EPHESIANS 3:20–21 AMP

God is able to do more than you think He can. In fact, He can do "superabundantly more"—infinitely beyond all of your prayers, hopes, and dreams. Does your view of God allow for such mystery and power?

C. S. Lewis once said, "My idea of God is a not divine idea. It has to be shattered from time to time. He shatters it Himself."

Ask God to show Himself to you in new ways, to shatter your human idea of Him. Be open to the work of the Holy Spirit in your heart.

Lord, I confess that my view of You is too small. Open my mind and my heart to believe that You are the God of miracles. Yesterday, today, and forever.

THE LORD OF HEAVEN'S ARMIES IS YOUR FATHER

"Be still, and know that I am God! I will be honored by every nation. I will be honored throughout the world." The Lord *of Heaven's Armies is here among us; the God of Israel is our fortress.*

Psalm 46:10–11 NLT

Praying to God is not about sending off your wish list to heaven and moving on with your day. It's about your relationship with the triune God. He wants to spend time with you as your friend, and He wants to comfort and advise you like a wise and loving parent. He wants you to know how much you are loved and protected.

The Lord of Heaven's Armies is your Father. He is with you, speaking to you, listening to you, and fighting your battles.

Sometimes sitting in the quiet with God is the best way to pray. Ask Him to fill you with His love as you sit quietly in His presence. Picture yourself climbing into God's lap and letting Him parent you. Or sitting with Him over coffee as you spend time together as friends. What does He want you to know today?

Lord, You can do anything. I'm so thankful that You're my Father!

PICTURE THIS

God made the earth by His power; He established the world by His wisdom and by His understanding and skill He has stretched out the heavens. When He utters His voice, there is a tumult of waters in the heavens, and He causes the clouds and the mist to ascend from the end of the earth; He makes lightning for the rain, and brings out the wind from His treasuries and from His storehouses.

JEREMIAH 10:12–13 AMP

Can you picture this scripture passage in your mind's eye? Can you imagine God stretching out the heavens? Can you see Him bringing out the wind from His treasure box?

This same Creator of all is your God! He cares about you like there is only one of you to care about. When you think about God's unlimited power and His unconditional love for you, what happens to your problems? Do you trust that God can handle anything going on in your life? Talk to Him about the problems on your mind currently. Ask Him to help!

Lord, You have my heart. I'm amazed at Your raw power and Your tender love for me.

THE BLESSING OF FRIENDSHIP WITH GOD

"I no longer call you servants, because a servant does not know his master's business. Instead, I have called you friends, for everything that I learned from my Father I have made known to you."
JOHN 15:15 NIV

For much of recorded history, a face-to-face friendship with God was not possible. In the Old Testament, we see that only a few chosen people were permitted a special friendship with God. In Exodus 33 we read that Moses was one of those special few. Verse 11 (NIV) says, "The LORD would speak to Moses face to face, as one speaks to a friend." But the others only looked on in awe and wonder. They weren't permitted this close relationship.

Now, because of all that Jesus has done for us on the cross, we are able to have a special, face-to-face friendship with God. It isn't something to take for granted. Jesus paid the ultimate price for this friendship. And God has chosen you to be His friend.

God, I'm honored and amazed that You call me Your friend because of Jesus. Help me never take it for granted.

A POWERFUL PERSPECTIVE

"It is He who spreads out the north over emptiness and hangs the earth on nothing. He wraps the waters in His clouds [which otherwise would spill on earth all at once], and the cloud does not burst under them. . . . Yet these are just the fringes of His ways [mere samples of His power], the faintest whisper of His voice! Who can contemplate the thunder of His [full] mighty power?"

JOB 26:7–8, 14 AMP

Reflect on the great power of God. Imagine Him creating the world and hanging the earth on nothing! And God's Word tells us this is just a mere sample of His full and mighty power. Only the faintest whisper of His voice.

How amazing that this all-powerful Creator God has His thoughts set on you. He loves you more than you could ever understand. Ask Him to help you hear His voice. Be listening for Him in all of creation. Notice how this outlook changes your perspective about your life and your circumstances.

Lord, nothing is out of Your realm of possibility. I trust Your Word that You care about everything in my life. Please give me Your perspective.

DAY AFTER DAY AFTER DAY

"I'll be with you as you do this, day after day after day, right up to the end of the age."
MATTHEW 28:20 MSG

When God became man, everything changed. We no longer have to worship in temples built by human hands. His Word tells us that His temple is now right in our very own hearts. He takes up residence there and has promised to be with us always, through everything. Day after day after day.

He is with you now in whatever circumstance you are facing. He sees you. He cares about your heart and the things that weigh you down. You don't have to carry anything alone any longer.

If you are going through a dark valley, open God's Word to Psalm 23. Prayerfully picture how Jesus wants to care for you.

I trust in Your promises, Lord God. I am confident that You will do what You say You're going to do! I accept the truth that Your goodness, mercy, and unfailing love will cover me all the days of my life. Now and for all eternity.

LONG FOR HIS PRESENCE

Give thanks to the LORD and proclaim his greatness. Let the whole world know what he has done. Sing to him; yes, sing his praises. Tell everyone about his wonderful deeds. Exult in his holy name; rejoice, you who worship the LORD. Search for the LORD and for his strength; continually seek him.

1 CHRONICLES 16:8–11 NLT

Begin your day with a prayer of thanksgiving for all God has done. Commit to making this day a day of praise and thanksgiving, regardless of your schedule. Ask Him to help you keep a thankful heart throughout your work today.

Verse 11 in the Amplified Bible says, "Seek the LORD and His strength; seek His face continually [longing to be in His presence]." Ask for God's supernatural power to remind you that you can choose to welcome God into every moment, every task, every meeting, every thought. If you struggle with longing to be in His presence, ask Him to give you that desire today.

Lord, plant in me a deep longing for Your presence, Your thoughts, Your love.

PRAYER BLESSINGS

Pray also for me, that whenever I speak,
words may be given me so that I will fearlessly
make known the mystery of the gospel.
EPHESIANS 6:19 NIV

We know that prayer is powerful. The apostle Paul asked for prayer and prayed regularly for his brothers and sisters in Christ. You can bless others with your prayers in powerful ways.

Second Corinthians 13:9, 11 (NLT) says: "We pray that you will become mature. . . . Be joyful. Grow to maturity. Encourage each other. Live in harmony and peace. Then the God of love and peace will be with you."

Humbly offering prayers for your brothers and sisters in Christ is a habit that can transform lives. Pray for your leaders, your pastors and teachers, any missionaries your church might support, your friends and family, and finally for yourself.

Ask God to complete the work He started in you (Philippians 1:6). Ask Him to help you grow in maturity and godly character. Pray that He would give you courage to share the love of Jesus with the people in your life.

Lord, I lift up my fellow believers around the world. Please finish what You started in us.

THE BLESSING OF LIGHT

For at one time you were darkness, but now you are light in the Lord. Walk as children of light.
EPHESIANS 5:8 ESV

Take a look at what the Bible says about light:

- "The true light that gives light to everyone was coming into the world" (John 1:9 NIV).
- "Again Jesus spoke to them, saying, 'I am the light of the world. Whoever follows me will not walk in darkness, but will have the light of life'" (John 8:12 ESV).
- "For you are all children of light, children of the day" (1 Thessalonians 5:5 ESV).

Jesus, the true light, came to rid people of darkness. He offers that same light to you. As God's beloved daughter and a follower of Jesus, you are a child of light. Do you think of yourself in this way? Ask the Holy Spirit to remind you of this truth and to help you accept it in your heart. Picture yourself bringing God's light into dark places.

Light of the world, thank You for planting Your light in my heart. Help me to walk in Your ways and carry Your light with me wherever I go.

EXPECTING PEACE

"Peace I leave with you; my peace I give you. I do not give to you as the world gives. Do not let your hearts be troubled and do not be afraid."
JOHN 14:27 NIV

This world advertises peace by way of luxury vacations and problem-free living. But that's not the kind of peace Jesus offers. In John 16:33 (AMP), Jesus says, "'I have told you these things, so that in Me you may have [perfect] peace. In the world you have tribulation and distress and suffering, but be courageous [be confident, be undaunted, be filled with joy]; I have overcome the world.' [My conquest is accomplished, My victory abiding.]"

We can't expect this life to be heaven, because it's not. The perfect peace that Jesus offers consists of His presence and His power in the midst of problems.

Do you need to let go of your expectations of what this world should be? Embrace the reality and goodness of God's peace and presence in the midst of a dark world.

Lord Jesus, You have overcome this world. My hope is in You. Fill me with the peace of Your presence.

HUMBLE PRAYERS

I will bow down [in worship] toward Your holy temple and give thanks to Your name for Your lovingkindness and Your truth; for You have magnified Your word together with Your name. On the day I called, You answered me; and You made me bold and confident with [renewed] strength in my life.

PSALM 138:2–3 AMP

People have always bowed or knelt before kings and queens to show their respect. God's Word tells us that Jesus knelt to pray sometimes too. Our freedom in Christ grants us the privilege to pray anytime, in any place, about anything. No rituals are needed any longer.

But sometimes, as the Spirit leads you, you may choose to pray humbly on your knees. Consider praying this way today. Find a quiet place and kneel before your King. Bring everything on your heart to God in prayer. Allow this act of praise and worship to strengthen your faith and give you courage to rise to meet the day's challenges.

Lord, I bow before You, humbly acknowledging You as my God and King. I want to serve You well, with Your Spirit guiding me in everything.

BLESSING YOUR BODY

Don't be concerned about the outward beauty of fancy hairstyles, expensive jewelry, or beautiful clothes. You should clothe yourselves instead with the beauty that comes from within, the unfading beauty of a gentle and quiet spirit, which is so precious to God.

1 PETER 3:3–4 NLT

God gave you your body purposefully. You devalue God's creation when you turn from your mirror in disgust. It's time to bless your body.

Stand in front of a full-length mirror and ask God for help to accept yourself and your body just the way He made you. Ask Him to be with you and speak truth to you as you bless every part of your body. Start at your feet and work your way up. Thank Him specifically for every part of your amazing body. Ask Him to continue blessing your body with health and strength.

Instead of feeling defeated by the flaws you see, ask God to help you take good care of the body He gave you, and trust in faith that He will.

Creator God, help me to see myself as You see me and to take care of my body well.

THE POWER OF A NAME

For to us a child is born, to us a son is given, and the government will be on his shoulders. And he will be called Wonderful Counselor, Mighty God, Everlasting Father, Prince of Peace.

Isaiah 9:6 niv

There is power in the name of Jesus. Knowing and praying the names of Jesus can be a powerful form of worship. Jesus is called many names throughout scripture, and learning these names helps us understand what kind of God we serve.

Isaiah tells us first that Jesus is called the Wonderful Counselor. He holds all the wisdom and knowledge we could ever need. Colossians 2:3 (nlt) tells us, "In him lie hidden all the treasures of wisdom and knowledge."

Jesus has the perfect answer for every one of your questions. Thank Him for His wonderful knowledge. Ask Him to give you wisdom as you seek Him every day.

Your names mean so much to me, Jesus. I praise You for being my Wonderful Counselor. You offer everything my heart desires and all the wisdom I need to live my life in victory.

JESUS, MIGHTY GOD

"I will be a Father to you, and you will be my sons and daughters, says the Lord Almighty."
2 CORINTHIANS 6:18 NIV

Jesus is your Mighty God. He is a warrior, able to fight all of your battles. Take a look at these scriptures that tell of the greatness of God:

- "Great is our [majestic and mighty] Lord and abundant in strength; His understanding is inexhaustible [infinite, boundless]" (Psalm 147:5 AMP).
- "All this also comes from the LORD Almighty, whose plan is wonderful, whose wisdom is magnificent" (Isaiah 28:29 NIV).
- "For the LORD your God is he who goes with you to fight for you against your enemies, to give you the victory" (Deuteronomy 20:4 ESV).

When you call upon the name of the Almighty, you are declaring His greatness and power. In what situation do you need God to fight for you? Where do you need Him to shield and protect you?

Jesus, You are my almighty God. I believe You can fight for me in all of my battles. You are bigger than anything I come against. Nothing is a match for Your power and greatness.

JESUS, EVERLASTING FATHER

"Let the children come to me. Don't stop them! For the Kingdom of Heaven belongs to those who are like these children."

MATTHEW 19:14 NLT

In Isaiah 9:6 Jesus is called our Everlasting Father. As Jesus welcomed the little children to come to Him, so He welcomes you.

Why is Jesus, the Son of God, called our Everlasting Father? A quick look into His character in scripture, and you'll understand why. He is fatherly in how He treats us. He treats us as a good father treats his children.

Can you picture yourself climbing onto the lap of Jesus and letting Him love you like a good and perfect father? Allow Jesus to meet all the "father" needs in your heart. He can fill the empty spaces that no earthly father ever could.

Jesus, I pray that You would heal any father wounds in my heart. Fill me like only You can. Thank You for Your father's heart toward me. I love You, Lord Jesus.

JESUS, PRINCE OF PEACE

Therefore, since we have been made right in God's sight by faith, we have peace with God because of what Jesus Christ our Lord has done for us. Because of our faith, Christ has brought us into this place of undeserved privilege where we now stand, and we confidently and joyfully look forward to sharing God's glory.

Romans 5:1–2 NLT

Jesus is your Prince of Peace. His sacrifice was the only way possible for you to have peace with God. He wants to be your Prince of Peace in every moment, in every situation.

Philippians 4 reminds us that when we go to God in prayer about everything, something supernatural happens. Verse 7 (NLT) says, "Then you will experience God's peace, which exceeds anything we can understand. His peace will guard your hearts and minds as you live in Christ Jesus."

Where do you need to experience the peace of Christ in your life? Bring all of your cares to Jesus.

Jesus, my heart is heavy over several things. I bring them to You in prayer. I need Your peace to permeate my heart and mind.

BLESSING GOD

Bless and affectionately praise the LORD, O my soul, and all that is [deep] within me, bless His holy name. Bless and affectionately praise the LORD, O my soul, and do not forget any of His benefits.

PSALM 103:1–2 AMP

The Bible, and especially the book of Psalms, frequently encourages us to bless God. Take a look:

- "I bless GOD every chance I get; my lungs expand with his praise" (Psalm 34:1 MSG).
- "Bless the LORD, O my soul, and all that is within me, bless his holy name! Bless the LORD, O my soul, and forget not all his benefits, who forgives all your iniquity, who heals all your diseases, who redeems your life from the pit, who crowns you with steadfast love and mercy, who satisfies you with good so that your youth is renewed like the eagle's" (Psalm 103:1–5 ESV).
- "I will bless the LORD who has counseled me; indeed, my heart (mind) instructs me in the night" (Psalm 16:7 AMP).

Consider how you can bless the heart of God today.

Lord, I bless Your name with my words and deeds today. I honor You in my heart.

LET GOD SPEAK

Don't try to figure out everything on your own. Listen for GOD's voice in everything you do, everywhere you go; he's the one who will keep you on track.

PROVERBS 3:5–6 MSG

God wants you to be listening for His voice and following His ways in everything you do and everywhere you go. He is a speaking God, and He will confirm what He's saying to you. God doesn't make you guess if something you're hearing is from Him or not. When He wants you to know or do something specifically, you can count on Him to confirm it.

When God speaks, what He says will always line up with His Word. And He can speak to you in countless ways, if you're listening. You can hear Him in creation. You can hear Him in song. You can hear Him in prayer. You can hear Him in scripture. God can speak through anything (even a donkey in Numbers 22!) if you have ears to hear.

Lord, I want to get to know Your voice well. Please open my ears to hear.

THE BLESSING OF FORGIVENESS: PART 1

Be kind and helpful to one another, tender-hearted [compassionate, understanding], forgiving one another [readily and freely], just as God in Christ also forgave you.

EPHESIANS 4:32 AMP

Corrie ten Boom once said, "Forgiveness is an act of the will, and the will can function regardless of the temperature of the heart." If you know anything about Corrie's story (look it up!), you know she had a lot to forgive!

There is so much blessing in forgiveness. And you can choose to forgive even when you don't feel like it.

We ask forgiveness from God when we sin because our sin breaks fellowship with Him. When we come to Him and confess our sins, our relationship is restored quickly. God wants us to forgive others just as quickly, because when we carry around unforgiveness, it really gets in our way. Ask God for help to forgive the people who have wronged you.

Lord, please search my heart. I ask forgiveness for my wrong thinking and actions. Thank You for helping me to forgive Your way—readily and freely—so I don't carry around a bunch of burdens that I'm not meant to carry.

THE BLESSING OF FORGIVENESS: PART 2

Let all bitterness and wrath and anger and clamor [perpetual animosity, resentment, strife, fault-finding] and slander be put away from you, along with every kind of malice [all spitefulness, verbal abuse, malevolence].

EPHESIANS 4:31 AMP

Forgiveness and reconciliation are not the same thing. While we can forgive someone for hurting us, it won't always result in reconciliation of the relationship. When we forgive, we release someone from what they've done to us or against us. We no longer hold a grudge. In forgiveness, only one person needs to take part—the person doing the forgiving.

If someone has wronged you severely, you are not required to trust that person again. But with God's help, you can forgive them. Forgiveness means you leave the judgment and punishment in God's hands.

Lord, please give me wisdom in relationships where I've been hurt badly. Show me Your will and Your way.

PRACTICE LISTENING

Do not merely listen to the word, and so deceive yourselves. Do what it says. Anyone who listens to the word but does not do what it says is like someone who looks at his face in a mirror and, after looking at himself, goes away and immediately forgets what he looks like.

James 1:22–24 NIV

The Bible tells us that someone who is good at listening to God listens for His voice and then does what He says.

Start a prayer journal (if you don't have one already) and practice listening. Direct your thoughts to Jesus and His Word. Let Him lead and guide you to what He wants you to know today. Prayerfully write down all the ways He is directing you. It may be a special scripture or a worship song or a reminder of a message you heard at church. Then ask Him to confirm it. How does He want you to put this insight or teaching into action? Ask Him to reveal this to you.

Lord, Your Word tells me that You want me to be able to hear Your voice. I accept this truth in faith.

THE LIGHT THAT WILL NEVER GO OUT

In the beginning the Word already existed. The Word was with God, and the Word was God. He existed in the beginning with God. God created everything through him, and nothing was created except through him. The Word gave life to everything that was created, and his life brought light to everyone. The light shines in the darkness, and the darkness can never extinguish it.

John 1:1–5 NLT

God's Word tells us that the darkness can never extinguish the light. That's a blessing and a promise. The life of Jesus brought us this light, and it is what resides now in our hearts. Shining light in the darkness has always been God's plan. And you are part of it.

Ask for boldness, strength, and guidance to carry His light into the dark. His light will never be put out.

Lord, You are the light that has brought me out of darkness. Thank You for Your promise that the darkness can never extinguish Your light. Strengthen and embolden me to carry Your light into all the places You want me to go.

LET GOD HANDLE THE DETAILS

This is my life work: helping people understand and respond to this Message. It came as a sheer gift to me, a real surprise, God handling all the details. When it came to presenting the Message to people who had no background in God's way, I was the least qualified of any of the available Christians. God saw to it that I was equipped, but you can be sure that it had nothing to do with my natural abilities.

EPHESIANS 3:7–8 MSG

Paul said that his life's work was to help people understand and respond to the gospel of Jesus Christ. Paul didn't feel qualified or equipped, and the fact that God called him to do this was a real surprise and a gift to Paul.

If you feel like you've been put in a position that is beyond your natural abilities, you can trust that God always provides the tools you need to succeed. He will show up when you depend on His strength, allowing Him to handle the details.

Lord, I trust that if You've called me into a situation that feels beyond what I can do, You'll handle the details.

THE BEATITUDES

"God blesses those who are poor and realize their need for him, for the Kingdom of Heaven is theirs. God blesses those who mourn, for they will be comforted. God blesses those who are humble, for they will inherit the whole earth. God blesses those who hunger and thirst for justice, for they will be satisfied. God blesses those who are merciful, for they will be shown mercy. God blesses those whose hearts are pure, for they will see God. God blesses those who work for peace, for they will be called the children of God. God blesses those who are persecuted for doing right, for the Kingdom of Heaven is theirs."

MATTHEW 5:3–10 NLT

We see people asking for God's blessing throughout the entire Bible. When we ask for His blessing, we are asking for His purpose and power in our lives. . .not asking Him to give us everything we want.

The Beatitudes, shown above from Matthew 5, tell how to be blessed in God's kingdom. As you read through the Beatitudes, do you recognize any areas where you need God to work within your life?

Lord, I ask for Your blessing. I want Your purpose and power to prevail in my life.

THE BLESSING OF BREAD

Jesus said to them, "I am the Bread of Life.
He who comes to Me will never be hungry.
He who puts his trust in Me will never be thirsty."
John 6:35 NLV

In Bible times, daily bread was a necessity. Women spent hours every day making enough bread for their family for one day. Bread was vital to survival. The actual work of making the bread was even a blessing for those who viewed it as such as they prayed and worked out frustrations while kneading the dough.

Jesus says He is our Bread of Life. Just as the people of ancient times had to make fresh bread every day, Jesus wants us to come to Him every day. Without receiving spiritual food from Jesus, we cannot grow in our faith. As we come to Him daily for nourishment, He meets all of our needs.

Jesus, I do believe that You are the only one who can meet all of my needs, physical and spiritual. Thank You for Your never-ending supply.

CONFIDENT RELIANCE ON THE LORD

Trust in and rely confidently on the LORD with all your heart and do not rely on your own insight or understanding. In all your ways know and acknowledge and recognize Him, and He will make your paths straight and smooth [removing obstacles that block your way].

PROVERBS 3:5–6 AMP

A dear elderly friend of ours took this scripture to heart in every way. She would even talk to Jesus about the parking places she needed to be open for her when she drove to the grocery store. He cared because she cared.

Trusting God for everything takes practice and a simple, child-like trust that God can do anything. You never outgrow your need for this life skill.

When we forget that Jesus wants to help us make all of our decisions, we get confused and anxious. When we leave God out of the decision-making process, we open ourselves up to all kinds of unnecessary problems.

Confess any self-reliance to God in prayer. Repent and ask God to help transform your thinking in this area.

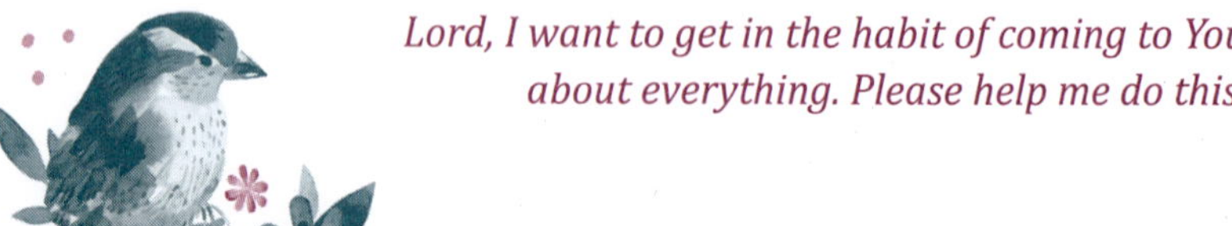

Lord, I want to get in the habit of coming to You about everything. Please help me do this.

WHEN YOU CAN'T FIX IT

Pile your troubles on God's shoulders—
he'll carry your load, he'll help you out.
He'll never let good people topple into ruin.
Psalm 55:22 msg

You were never meant to fix everything. Not even your own problems. Some difficulties just don't have good solutions that you can see. Reaching out to God in prayer is the best (and only) way to move forward.

"Lord, I just don't know what to do!" is a humble prayer that God can bless. He sees when you are in over your head. And He cares. He's the only one who can see everything from every angle.

Ask Jesus to help you discern His voice in your life and to make Himself clear to you. There is a next step. It may be to rest and trust. Or you may receive a clear directive in another way. Trust that God is faithful. He has good plans for you.

When you don't know what to do, wait on the Lord and pray. Trust Him to lead you and show you what He wants you to do in His timing.

Lord, I can't fix the situation I'm dealing with right now. I need Your help. Please show me what to do next.

REFLECTING GOD'S GLORY

Those who look to him are radiant;
their faces are never covered with shame.
PSALM 34:5 NIV

When you spend time with Jesus, He lights up everything about you: Your thoughts. Your heart. Your smile. People can tell when you've been with Him because you shine from being in His presence. You emanate peace because you've been enveloped in it.

Take a look at 2 Corinthians 3:18 (NLT): "So all of us who have had that veil removed can see and reflect the glory of the Lord. And the Lord—who is the Spirit—makes us more and more like him as we are changed into his glorious image."

Ask Jesus to give you a deep desire to be in His presence. And as He does, you'll begin to light up your world, reflecting the very glory of God Himself.

Lord, it's only because of You and through You that I can lift my head and reflect Your glory. Help me light the world around me with Your brilliance. Transform me into all You want me to be.

THE MASTER AT WORK

May God give you every good thing you need so you can do what He wants. May He do in us what pleases Him through Jesus Christ. May Christ have all the shining-greatness forever! Let it be so.

HEBREWS 13:21 NLV

God is at work in you. He is the master gardener, and He has a vested interest in growing His spiritual fruit in you. He will not leave before the harvest. The responsibility for your growth is not entirely on your shoulders. He has called you and He wants you to succeed.

You have the expert available to you at all times and in every way. He is carefully tending you in all the ways you've allowed Him access to the garden of your heart.

He is working with you to pull out weeds and facilitate new growth. He is nourishing you and watering you with living water. He will finish what He started (Philippians 1:6).

Lord, I give You full access to the garden of my heart. Please finish Your work in me. Show me how to better cooperate with Your process. Thank You for never giving up on me!

FAILING FORWARD

Don't interfere with good people's lives; don't try to get the best of them. No matter how many times you trip them up, God-loyal people don't stay down long; soon they're up on their feet, while the wicked end up flat on their faces.

PROVERBS 24:15–16 MSG

Jesus offers us grace upon grace. And yet we are incredibly hard on ourselves when we fail. Ask Jesus to help you see failure as a learning opportunity. Just take a look at some stories in the Bible, and you'll see example after example of God using failures for His greater purpose.

So what if you've failed? Give yourself some grace. As children, we learn the Golden Rule: Treat others as you want to be treated. But as adults, we often treat ourselves worse than anyone else.

You are God's precious child. He offers you His steadying hand every time you stumble. Lighten up on yourself as you learn to fail forward.

Lord, I repent of being harder on myself than I should be. Help me to be gracious with myself in my failures. Thanks for using me despite—and sometimes maybe even because of—them.

FULLY LOVED

He did this to show us through all the time to come the great riches of His loving-favor. He has shown us His kindness through Christ Jesus.

EPHESIANS 2:7 NLV

John Newton, who wrote the words to "Amazing Grace," said, "God often takes a course for accomplishing His purposes directly contrary to what our narrow views would prescribe. He brings a death upon our feelings, wishes and prospects when He is about to give us the desires of our hearts."

God is so kind to us. He sees the beginning and the end, and He knows exactly what we need to get us to where He wants us to go. He wants to bless us with joy as we experience an abundant and adventurous life with Him.

God wants you to live your life knowing that you are loved and cherished. You are the sparkle in His eye. You are the one He goes after when you've veered off the narrow path. He cares deeply for you.

Do you trust His heart for you?

Lord, I want to believe how fully I'm loved by You. Help me to live with this truth in freedom and victory.

THE SPARROW

"What is the price of two sparrows—one copper coin? But not a single sparrow can fall to the ground without your Father knowing it. And the very hairs on your head are all numbered. So don't be afraid; you are more valuable to God than a whole flock of sparrows."

MATTHEW 10:29–31 NLT

Civilla Martin wrote the hymn "His Eye Is on the Sparrow" after meeting a husband and wife who deeply loved God despite one being wheelchair-bound and the other being bedridden. They encouraged others and lived happily devoted to Christ despite their constant health struggles. When they were asked what gave them their hopefulness, the response was simply: "His eye is on the sparrow, and I know He watches me."

This matter-of-fact reply inspired Martin to write the famous words:

Why should I feel discouraged, why should the shadows come,
Why should my heart be lonely, and long for heaven and home,
When Jesus is my portion? My constant friend is He:
His eye is on the sparrow, and I know He watches me.

In peace I will lie down and sleep, for you alone, O LORD, will keep me safe (Psalm 4:8 NLT).

THE VICTOR'S CROWN

Everyone who runs in a race does many things so his body will be strong. He does it to get a crown that will soon be worth nothing, but we work for a crown that will last forever.
1 Corinthians 9:25 NLV

An eternal perspective on life helps us get through every trial. By faith, we know that our troubles are light and momentary, "achieving for us an eternal glory that far outweighs them all" (2 Corinthians 4:17 NIV).

This too shall pass. Every hard season does. Charles Spurgeon said, "There are no crown-bearers in heaven that were not cross-bearers here below." We press on because Jesus is with us.

James 1:12 (AMP) tells us, "Blessed [happy, spiritually prosperous, favored by God] is the man who is steadfast under trial and perseveres when tempted; for when he has passed the test and been approved, he will receive the [victor's] crown of life which the Lord has promised to those who love Him."

As we keep our eyes fixed on Jesus, He promises life now and life forever.

Lord, I know my struggles are temporary. Please fill me with Your strength to endure.

Where Does Strength Come From?

I look up to the mountains; does my strength come from mountains? No, my strength comes from God, who made heaven, and earth, and mountains.

Psalm 121:1–2 msg

Courage and strength to face this world don't come by digging down deep and tapping into your own resources. That's where exhaustion comes from. Supernatural strength and courage come from God alone. He is the very source of life and power.

Verses 7–8 (msg) of this psalm say, "God guards you from every evil, he guards your very life. He guards you when you leave and when you return, he guards you now, he guards you always."

God sees you. He knows your deep need. You are not alone in any battle.

Does this mean you can stop trying to manipulate circumstances and people to protect yourself? Yes. God is your guardian and protector. He will give you the courage and strength to do whatever it is He is asking of you. And sometimes it is simply to rest in Him.

You are my source of courage and strength, Lord. Help me rest in that truth.

GOD VALUES WOMEN

Deborah, the wife of Lappidoth, was a prophet who was judging Israel at that time. She would sit under the Palm of Deborah, between Ramah and Bethel in the hill country of Ephraim, and the Israelites would go to her for judgment.

JUDGES 4:4–5 NLT

This account in the Bible is surprising in a time when women were seen as little more than slaves in many cultures. Deborah was a wise, God-fearing woman. People flocked to her to hear her advice. She became one of the judges over all of Israel. She urged the Jewish people to repent and turn back to God.

God greatly values women and gifts them with ministry skills. God set Deborah up as a judge over both men and women. She commanded an army to go into battle and God gave them victory.

Let this biblical account bless you. God has great plans for you as a woman. You may not lead a militia, but you will be called into battle. And God is with you and for you.

Father God, I will follow where You lead, even if it seems beyond my capabilities. . .because You are with me.

WHOM SHALL I FEAR?

The Lord is my light and my salvation—
whom shall I fear? The Lord is the stronghold
of my life—of whom shall I be afraid?
Psalm 27:1 NIV

Intimidation is a common feeling. Certain people and situations can trigger a mild panic or fear in many people. But God says you don't have to feel that way. Knowing who you really are in Christ gives you supernatural strength and courage that you never had before, in any and every situation.

If you struggle with anxiety over other people's thoughts or opinions of you or consider yourself a shy person who fears standing up for herself or others. . .this is great news for you! Get into God's Word and uncover the truth of who you are in Christ. Ask the Holy Spirit to teach you and remind you of all these truths. You are a royal daughter of the King of all kings. You can hold your head high because you are God's child.

Lord, when I feel less-than around certain people, remind me that I am Yours. Give me the courage to speak up as You lead me.

VICTORY THROUGH WORSHIP

You are my hiding place; you will protect me from trouble and surround me with songs of deliverance.
Psalm 32:7 NIV

Worshipping God in the midst of hard times is incredibly powerful. Singing and praising God during trouble is a leap of faith. It shows that you are committed to trusting that God will make a way for you when it looks like there isn't one.

Isaiah 12:2 (NLT) says, "See, God has come to save me. I will trust in him and not be afraid. The Lord God is my strength and my song; he has given me victory."

The next time you feel like running away from your problems, hide out in Jesus instead. Compile a list of your favorite worship songs, songs that speak of God's faithfulness and power, and play them on repeat. Thank God for His songs of deliverance as you move forward in faith. Watch and see what He will do.

Jesus, I trust that You see me and know my heart. I worship You during this hard time, knowing that You will make a way for me.

WHEN GOD SAYS NO

But he said to me, "My grace is sufficient for you, for my power is made perfect in weakness." Therefore I will boast all the more gladly of my weaknesses, so that the power of Christ may rest upon me. For the sake of Christ, then, I am content with weaknesses, insults, hardships, persecutions, and calamities. For when I am weak, then I am strong.

2 CORINTHIANS 12:9–10 ESV

God loves to say yes to our prayers offered in faith. But sometimes He says no, just like a wise and loving parent would do, for a very good reason.

The apostle Paul had some sort of physical affliction (see verses 7–8). He begged God several times to take it away. But God said no. Why would He do that? Paul says that God did it to keep him reliant on God's power so that he wouldn't become conceited and proud.

Do you trust that God knows what is best for you, even when you receive a no?

Jesus, help me to be content in my weakness, allowing Your strength to shine through. Guard my heart against discouragement and help me trust You no matter what.

Seated with Christ in Heaven

It's a wonder God didn't lose his temper and do away with the whole lot of us. Instead, immense in mercy and with an incredible love, he embraced us. He took our sin-dead lives and made us alive in Christ. He did all this on his own, with no help from us! Then he picked us up and set us down in highest heaven in company with Jesus, our Messiah.

Ephesians 2:6 MSG

We all need Jesus. We've sinned so much. God could've just given up on the whole lot of us. But for some mysterious reason, God decided we were worth the greatest sacrifice. The Amplified Bible explains that when we believed, we were raised with Christ, and God "seated us with Him in the heavenly places, [because we are] in Christ Jesus."

The Bible says that this is our current position. Not a "when you die and go to heaven" position. There is no longer any reason to walk around in defeat! Your position in Christ is secure.

Jesus, I believe what You say is true. Help me to live my daily life like I believe it.

BORN OF GOD

Yet to all who did receive him, to those who believed in his name, he gave the right to become children of God—children born not of natural descent, nor of human decision or a husband's will, but born of God.

JOHN 1:12–13 NIV

Take a look at these scriptures:

- "Everyone who believes that Jesus is the Christ has been born of God, and everyone who loves the Father loves whoever has been born of him" (1 John 5:1 ESV).
- "We know that anyone born of God does not continue to sin; the One who was born of God keeps them safe, and the evil one cannot harm them" (1 John 5:18 NIV).

The Amplified Bible explains what being born of God means: "a divine and supernatural birth—they are born of God—spiritually transformed, renewed, sanctified" (John 1:13). This supernatural truth is more binding than your physical reality.

In Christ, you are God's child with rights to His full inheritance. You are born into His family.

I choose to believe Your Word, God. I'm Your child. I will live with gratitude in my heart for all You've done.

LIGHT BEARERS

"Here's another way to put it: You're here to be light, bringing out the God-colors in the world. God is not a secret to be kept. We're going public with this, as public as a city on a hill. If I make you light-bearers, you don't think I'm going to hide you under a bucket, do you? I'm putting you on a light stand. Now that I've put you there on a hilltop, on a light stand—shine! Keep open house; be generous with your lives. By opening up to others, you'll prompt people to open up with God, this generous Father in heaven."

MATTHEW 5:14–16 MSG

Where does God want you to shine forth His colorful light in the world? How can you be more generous to the people He has put in your life?

God has put you in certain circumstances and areas to be His light in the darkness. Don't be intimidated when things look bleak. You are right where you are for a season and a reason.

Keep the faith in the dark! God is at work, shining His light through you.

Jesus, please give me the courage to shine Your light in the dark.

WISDOM FOR LIFE

Keep vigilant watch over your heart; that's where life starts. Don't talk out of both sides of your mouth; avoid careless banter, white lies, and gossip. Keep your eyes straight ahead; ignore all sideshow distractions. Watch your step, and the road will stretch out smooth before you. Look neither right nor left; leave evil in the dust.

PROVERBS 4:23–27 MSG

Setting and keeping good boundaries is a wise spiritual discipline. It's not your job to fix other people or keep them happy. You are responsible to God for yourself and your own choices, as is everyone else.

"Guarding your heart" is not meant to be a selfish endeavor. It's okay to prayerfully say no. And also to be considerate and prayerful before you say yes. God has a plan and a purpose for you. He gives you the specific resources to carry out that plan. Your yeses and nos to other people can hinder that process, depleting those precious resources, if you don't stay vigilant.

Lord, help me to be wise with the time and resources You've given me. Show me how to have healthy boundaries that honor You.

THE BLESSING OF REPENTANCE

"Repent, then, and turn to God, so that your sins may be wiped out, that times of refreshing may come from the Lord."
ACTS 3:19 NIV

Jesus calls us to return to God. Day by day and hour by hour. Only as we exchange our will for His can we find the true blessing of His mercy and grace.

In the words of Amy Carmichael:

And shall I pray Thee change Thy will, my Father,
Until it be according unto mine?
But, no, Lord, no, that never shall be, rather
I pray Thee blend my human will with Thine.

Are you longing to rest in God's mercy and grace? Bring your whole self to Him. Hold nothing back. You will be blessed and free.

I come to You, Lord Jesus, with all of my heart.

YOUR STORY IS A BLESSING

A happy heart makes the face cheerful,
but heartache crushes the spirit.
PROVERBS 15:13 NIV

Author and theologian Frederick Buechner said that he used to believe he couldn't be happy unless the people he loved were happy too. But he came to change his way of thinking when he realized that, through our own stories, we can positively impact the lives of others. He said that we have the right to be happy—in fact, a duty to be happy. Even in hard times, we can find joy that will help us learn and grow. And, if we keep listening, God will speak to us and show us how we can use our stories to influence our friends, family, and neighbors.

Reflect on your life, the sad and the happy, the good and the bad. Consider how God can use all of your experiences to bless you and the people He has put in your life.

Lord, I want to learn and grow through everything.
Please use my story to help someone else.

FREELY AND LIGHTLY

"Therefore do not worry about tomorrow, for tomorrow will worry about itself. Each day has enough trouble of its own."
MATTHEW 6:34 NIV

Humans love to plan and prepare. Creating and designing with anticipation is a good thing. It's when we let worry creep in that planning becomes a problem. We were never meant to carry tomorrow's load. Doing so causes undue stress and robs today of precious time and joy.

When you worry about tomorrow, you are allowing yourself to believe that God won't come through for you or that He's not able to handle your problems. Repent of worry. Jesus wants you to have an abundant life (John 10:10). Take a look at Matthew 11:28–30 in The Message. The last verse says: "Keep company with me and you'll learn to live freely and lightly."

Lord, I'm sorry for not trusting You with my tomorrows. Help me believe that You'll give me the resources and strength for each day.

GOD'S UNFAILING LOVE

Let the morning bring me word of your unfailing love, for I have put my trust in you. Show me the way I should go, for to you I entrust my life.
PSALM 143:8 NIV

God's love for you will never fail. He reminds us of this truth over and over in His Word. Take a look:

- "In your unfailing love you will lead the people you have redeemed. In your strength you will guide them to your holy dwelling" (Exodus 15:13 NIV).
- "But I trust in your unfailing love; my heart rejoices in your salvation" (Psalm 13:5 NIV).
- "For the king trusts in the LORD; through the unfailing love of the Most High he will not be shaken" (Psalm 21:7 NIV).
- "Many are the woes of the wicked, but the LORD's unfailing love surrounds the one who trusts in him" (Psalm 32:10 NIV).

And those are just a few. God wants you to know and believe that He will never ever fail you. People were never meant to be your savior. Let God be God in your life.

Lord Jesus, satisfy me with Your unfailing love.

THE BLESSING OF LAUGHTER

And now, God, do it again—bring rains to our drought-stricken lives so those who planted their crops in despair will shout "Yes!" at the harvest, so those who went off with heavy hearts will come home laughing, with armloads of blessing.

Psalm 126:4–6 msg

Much research has been done on the act of laughing. Science has determined that it is healing for your body to laugh. Laughter releases endorphins, reduces stress, and increases the chemicals in your body that make you feel good.

Studies also show that joyful laughing can literally protect your heart! One researcher found that laughter acts as an anti-inflammatory.

Having a good sense of humor is a gift from God. If you've been in a season where joyful laughter hasn't been bubbling up as much, bring your sorrows to Jesus. Be patient with yourself and ask God to keep healing your heart, restoring your laughter in His time.

Jesus, I want to laugh again. I bring You my brokenness and ask that my heavy heart be made light by You.

JESUS IN DISGUISE

"'When did we ever see you hungry and feed you, thirsty and give you a drink? And when did we ever see you sick or in prison and come to you?' Then the King will say, 'I'm telling the solemn truth: Whenever you did one of these things to someone overlooked or ignored, that was me—you did it to me.'"

MATTHEW 25:39–40 MSG

The way we treat people says everything about how we love Jesus. If you were raised by loving parents, you were treated with kindness and respect and taught to treat others the same way. Many people, however, were not raised in loving homes. They don't treat others well because they've never experienced such treatment themselves and simply don't know how to extend it.

God wants us to be on the lookout for the needs of others. The next time you're offended by the actions of others, ask Jesus to help you look deeper. A person who treats others poorly is likely deeply wounded. How can you show them the love of Jesus? As you love others, you are loving Jesus Himself.

Lord, help me see beyond the surface to the heart. Show me how to love the difficult ones.

GOD IS CRAZY ABOUT YOU

Therefore the LORD waits [expectantly] and longs to be gracious to you, and therefore He waits on high to have compassion on you. For the LORD is a God of justice; blessed (happy, fortunate) are all those who long for Him [since He will never fail them].

ISAIAH 30:18 AMP

Why would God do what He did for us? Because of love. He is a perfect and loving Father who would do anything for His kids.

Hannah Whitall Smith said, "Nothing can separate you from God's love—absolutely nothing. God is enough for time, God is enough for eternity. God is enough!"

He longs to be with you. He wants to bless you with goodness and compassion and grace. He is the only one who can! Spend some time praising Him and thanking Him for His gracious love today.

Lord God, I'm in awe of Your unfailing love for me. Give me a deep desire to know You and love You more.

CHRIST IS YOUR LIFE

Set your minds on things above, not on earthly things. For you died, and your life is now hidden with Christ in God. When Christ, who is your life, appears, then you also will appear with him in glory.

COLOSSIANS 3:2–4 NIV

Sometimes the weight of this world can be crushing. You get on social media to connect with friends and instead your heart becomes heavier for all kinds of reasons. Thankfully, our hope is in Jesus and He fully understands your conflicted emotions.

As you run to Him for safety and perspective, you can be sure that you are secure in Him. That's not just the hope of heaven someday. Jesus came so that you could have hope and peace and joy right now.

Bring those heavy emotions to Jesus and know that you are covered, made new, and completely safe in Christ. Now and forever. Lift your head. Pray for your friends. Move forward in faith and security.

Jesus, You are my life. You cover me and make me new. You give me confidence to live this life with an eternal perspective.

CONFIDENTLY EXPECTING THE LORD

Be strong and let your hearts take courage, all you who wait for and confidently expect the Lord.
Psalm 31:24 AMP

Is your personality naturally strong and courageous, or do you struggle with feeling weak and afraid? Or maybe you fall somewhere in the middle.

When you call on Jesus as the Lord of your life, you are declaring that He is your director, your coach, the boss of your life. You are surrendering your will for His. If you lack courage, He will give it to you. If you battle fear, He will fight for you. If you would rather do everything on your own, He can give you the desire to ask for help.

When you put your hope in the power and strength of the Lord, you can confidently expect Him to show up and keep His promises. As you are listening for His voice and walking in His ways, He will lead you everywhere you need to go.

Jesus, please be Lord over every area of my life. My confidence is in Your faithfulness.

A HEAVENLY MINDSET

"You will keep in perfect and constant peace the one whose mind is steadfast [that is, committed and focused on You—in both inclination and character], because he trusts and takes refuge in You [with hope and confident expectation]."

Isaiah 26:3 amp

When we focus our thoughts on Jesus, we can go into any circumstance or relationship with confidence that comes from setting our minds on things above.

As Colossians 3:1–2 (niv) reminds us, "Since, then, you have been raised with Christ, set your hearts on things above, where Christ is, seated at the right hand of God. Set your minds on things above, not on earthly things."

Will worrying about what other people think of you keep you in perfect peace? Nope, never. The next time you find yourself walking into a situation that causes worry, take a deep breath and pray. Take your thoughts captive. Picture yourself seated with Christ in heaven. Set your heart and mind on Jesus. Then move forward in His strength and purpose.

Lord Jesus, help me choose to take my thoughts captive. Please give me a heavenly mindset.

ASTONISHING TRUTH

No, in all these things we are more than conquerors through him who loved us. For I am convinced that neither death nor life, neither angels nor demons, neither the present nor the future, nor any powers, neither height nor depth, nor anything else in all creation, will be able to separate us from the love of God that is in Christ Jesus our Lord.

ROMANS 8:37–39 NIV

The truth of God's Word is astonishing to those of us who believe. We are free and made righteous in Christ. We are God's beloved and holy children. We are currently seated with Christ in the heavenlies. Nothing can separate us from the love of God.

If Christians lived out these truths every day, if they walked in the courage that Christ says is ours, it would change everything.

It can change everything.

It will change everything. . .if you believe it.

Jesus, I want to walk in Your truth every day. Forgive me for my unbelief at times. Give me the courage to trust Your Word.

TRANSFORMED BY PRAYER

About eight days after Jesus said this, he took Peter, John and James with him and went up onto a mountain to pray. As he was praying, the appearance of his face changed, and his clothes became as bright as a flash of lightning.

Luke 9:28–29 NIV

Prayer is transforming. Remember that 2 Corinthians 3:18 (NIV) tells us that we are all "being transformed into his image with ever-increasing glory, which comes from the Lord, who is the Spirit."

What happens during transformation? Pastor Robert Gelinas explains it this way: Transformation is "where God takes all of our past, the good and the bad, He wraps it all up in the cocoon of His love. After His love has done its work, you come out the other side with a life more beautiful than you could ever imagine."

This isn't only the promise of heaven. It's the work of the Spirit that Jesus wants to begin in you right now.

Jesus, please transform me as I get close to You. I submit to Your loving ways in my life. Do Your work in me.

MOMENT BY MOMENT WITH GOD

Seek the LORD and his strength; seek his presence continually!
1 CHRONICLES 16:11 ESV

God created you for relationship. His Spirit is alive in your heart, and as you grow in faith, you become more and more aware of His presence at work in you. You can choose to be in His presence continually.

What does this look like? As you interact with others, you can simultaneously bring them before God's throne in prayer. As you grocery shop, you can talk to God. As you work, you can pray for God's perspective and help. You can keep a song of thankfulness in your heart all day. You can live your life and do your activities all while being present with God at the same time.

God is with you always. He never leaves you. But you can become more aware of His presence in each moment.

Take some time to pray and ask God to give you a reminder that He is with you.

Jesus, I want to seek You more than I do. Remind me that You are with me always. Help me to become more aware of Your presence.

GRACIOUS AND PRAYERFUL

For now we see only a reflection as in a mirror;
then we shall see face to face. Now I know in part;
then I shall know fully, even as I am fully known.
1 CORINTHIANS 13:12 NIV

Often, pride prevents people from seeing things as they truly are. Especially people who don't see themselves as prideful. A false humility can even set in. But the truth is that we just don't know everything. Making quick judgments about people and situations is harmful in so many ways.

We can't see the big picture yet. We don't know all that God is doing in another person's journey. We don't know where they came from or the secret pain they've had to endure. We don't know why they say or do the things they say and do. Highly emotional or irrational responses from people are often caused by unresolved trauma.

So be gracious and prayerful as you go about relating to others. Be patient with yourself and others.

Lord, I confess I often judge too quickly.
Help me give and receive grace.

PRAYERS FOR FAMILY AND FRIENDS

Dear friend, I pray that you may enjoy good health and that all may go well with you, even as your soul is getting along well.

3 John 2 niv

Have you written out a prayer list lately? Take a few moments now to write out on paper your friends and family who need prayer. The Bible tells us that our prayers are powerful and effective (James 5:16). Taking just a few minutes a day to bless others in the name of Jesus can make a huge difference in the trajectory of their lives!

Tuck this prayer list in your Bible and keep updating it. Then let the people on your list know that you're praying over them. A little note of encouragement to that effect can help people know they aren't alone and that God cares. They may feel their load getting a little bit lighter knowing that someone else is carrying them before the throne of God.

Lord, I pray for ______________. You know everything they need. I pray that they would sense Your presence in their lives. That they would experience Your power in ways they didn't believe before.

HOPE FOR RECONCILIATION

But Joseph said to them, "Don't be afraid. Am I in the place of God? You intended to harm me, but God intended it for good to accomplish what is now being done, the saving of many lives. So then, don't be afraid. I will provide for you and your children." And he reassured them and spoke kindly to them.

GENESIS 50:19–21 NIV

God can heal the hurts of our past. The story of Joseph is proof of that. His siblings grew abusive toward him in response to his youthful arrogance about being his father's favorite. It took many years and a lot of humility and growing up for this story to unfold and for reconciliation to take place.

If you're in the middle of family or relational dysfunction, take hope. You can't fix it, but God can. Don't rush Him. You may want things fixed right now, but God takes His time. He has important lessons to teach in the waiting. Trust Him and His timing. He knows what He is doing.

Lord Jesus, I bring my broken relationships to You. I trust You and Your timing. I release my burdens into Your hands.

THE GIFT OF GRACE

For it is by grace [God's remarkable compassion and favor drawing you to Christ] that you have been saved [actually delivered from judgment and given eternal life] through faith. And this [salvation] is not of yourselves [not through your own effort], but it is the [undeserved, gracious] gift of God.

EPHESIANS 2:8 AMP

Have you ever been given an extravagant gift that made you feel uncomfortable? Or have you ever received a gift from a loved one that you didn't really want, yet you knew they would be excited to see you use it? Gift exchange can be very awkward.

Thankfully, God doesn't leave us in an awkward position. He gives us an extravagant gift and lets us know exactly what He wants us to do with it: Accept it. Use it. Simply love Him and others. That sums up everything God wants us to know in life (Matthew 22:37–40).

How will you use God's extravagant gift of grace in your life?

Jesus, I'm so amazed by how graciously You love me. Let that love overflow in me and spill out onto everyone around me.

A BEAUTIFUL LIFE PATH

For we are His workmanship [His own master work, a work of art], created in Christ Jesus [reborn from above—spiritually transformed, renewed, ready to be used] for good works, which God prepared [for us] beforehand [taking paths which He set], so that we would walk in them [living the good life which He prearranged and made ready for us].

EPHESIANS 2:10 AMP

You are God's glorious work of art. And as you bring your full self to God each day, being real before Him, allowing Him to share in your joys and sorrows, and submitting to His work in your life. . .you become spiritually transformed, renewed, and ready to be used.

God has beautiful plans for your life. He has a special path just for you. As you walk hand in hand with Jesus along His life-path, you will live the good life. . .now and for all eternity!

Jesus, thank You for taking my hand on this beautiful life-path You have set before me. I trust You. I love You. I will follow You.

SCRIPTURE INDEX

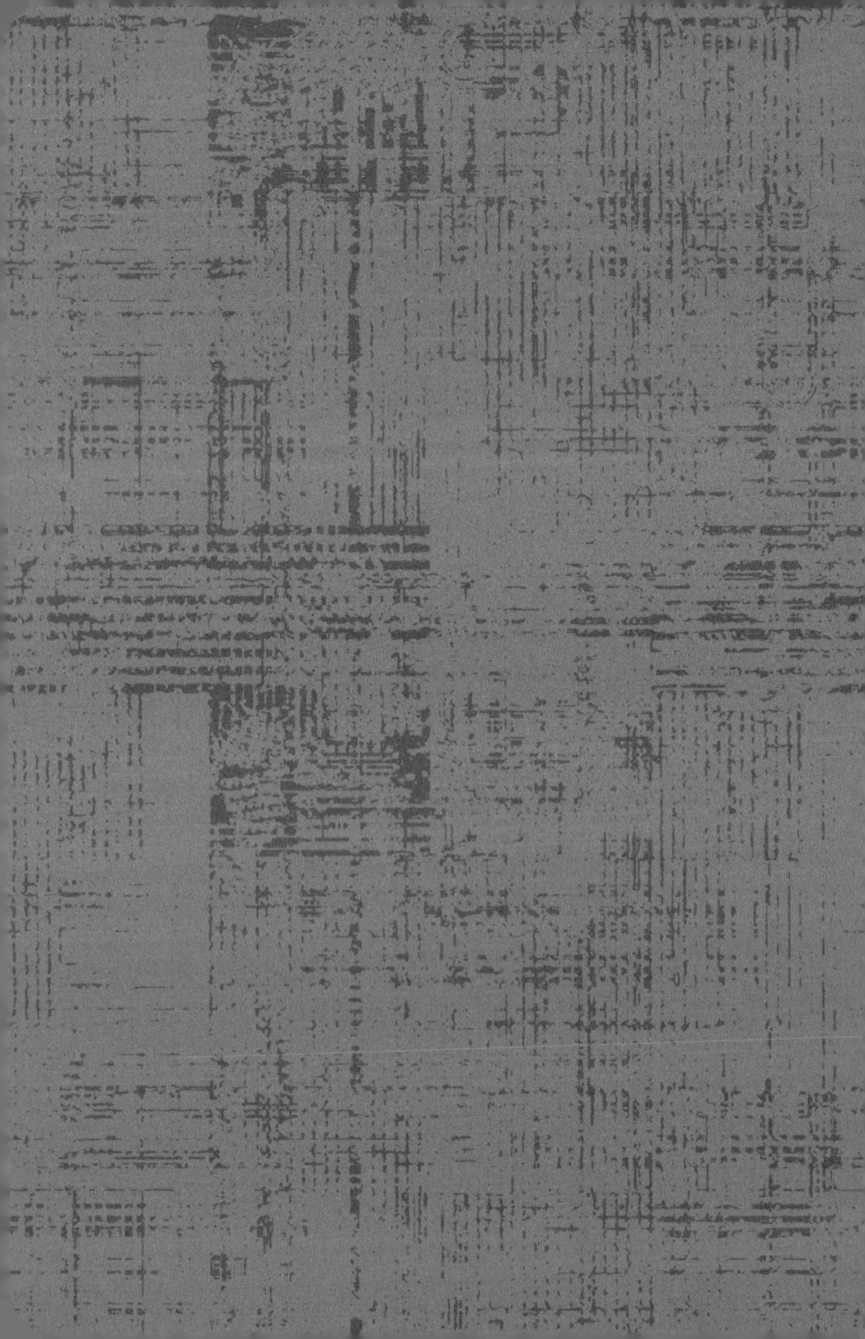